RISKING HUMAN SECURITY

RISKING HUMAN SECURITY

Attachment and Public Life

edited by
Marci Green

KARNAC

First published in 2008 by
Karnac Books Ltd
118 Finchley Road, London NW3 5HT

British Library Cataloguing in Publication Data

A C.I.P. for this book is available from the British Library

ISBN: 978 1 85575 597 0

Edited, designed and produced by The Studio Publishing Services Ltd
www.publishingservicesuk.co.uk
e-mail: studio@publishingservicesuk.co.uk

Printed in Great Britain

www.karnacbooks.com

CONTENTS

ACKNOWLEDGEMENTS

The ideas for this book developed over four years, and there are many people whose support helped shape its content and direction.

A grant from the Nuffield foundation enabled me to travel in the UK, the USA, and Italy, to consult published materials and confer with researchers, psychotherapists, political activists, and human rights workers. I am especially indebted to colleagues at the following institutions: in Boston and Cambridge, Massachusetts—the Francois-Xavier Bagnoud Center for Health and Human Rights; The Center for Health and Public Policy at Boston University, the Victims of Violence Program; the Central Street Health Clinic and Dr Beth Parsons, in particular; The American Friends Services Committee and, especially, Paul Shannon and Joseph Gerson; and Karlen Lyons-Ruth at Cambridge City Hospital. In Florence, I spent valuable time with researchers and fieldworkers at the Innocenti Research Centre (UNICEF). In Los Angeles, I had the opportunity to work with colleagues from the Los Angeles Attachment Study Group, especially Drs Diana Taylor and Robin Mintzer, whose attachment-sensitive work in communities provides a good model for enabling change.

Colleagues and friends, such as the staff in the School of Humanities, Languages and Social Science (HLSS) from Wolverhampton University have contributed in numerous ways to this project. Lesley Tennick, secretary for HLSS, helped administrate my research grant and travel arrangements. Her grace and good humour made difficult moments easier to manage. I am also thankful for the consistent support of Drs. Andrew Cooper, Associate Dean, Barbara Gwinnett, Dean, of HLSS and Pauline Anderson, Head of Sociology, who performed organizational magic to release me from teaching and provide financial assistance. Rachel Roland, from the CITRUS PROJECT, enabled me to co-ordinate, with the Los Angeles Group, a Symposium in Wolverhampton on "Attachment-sensitive interventions in the community" (co-funded by HLSS). Colleagues and friends, in Sociology—Shirin Housee, Paul Grant, Andrew Cameron, and Elaine Cameron—encouraged my work and allowed me to test my ideas in their classrooms, where I met some lively students: Kelly Walsh, Oliver Smith, Sarah Warde, and Jamie Gunn, whose interest in attachment theory fed my passion. In the USA, Lani and Joe Gerson, Linda Dittmar and Gordon Fellman were a constant source of good ideas and offered a secure base from which I could explore. In the UK, Gareth Austin and Richard Sealy helped to visually express the themes of this book, and I am grateful for their assistance in designing the book's cover.

And, of course, I want to thank the contributors to this book. We have worked as a community, with mutual regard and respect, throughout the project. Within that group, two people in particular, have played a pivotal role: Joan Woodward and Peter Marris have been my mentors in attachment theory for several years, and their insights into the political dimensions of attachment relationships have been invaluable to me. It is with great sadness that I realize Peter will not see the book's completion. He died in the summer of 2007. Despite his illness, he continued to provide such good counsel, and I hope this book does justice to his vision.

Elaine Arnold, PhD, trained as a teacher and taught in Trinidad before changing her career to psychiatric social work and specializing in child guidance. She taught on a Master's programme in Social Work at Goldsmith's College, University of London and Sussex University (UK). She was a founding member of Nafsiyat Intercultural Therapy Centre, and worked as a counsellor before becoming its Director of Training. She has researched the effects on children and mothers of separation, loss, and reunion, as they arise from the migration experience. She founded the Separation and Reunion Forum, which works to raise awareness of the significance of separation and loss across the life span.

Jack Cole, doctoral candidate of the University of Massachusetts, is co-founder and executive director of Law Enforcement Against Prohibition. An international speaker, Jack has presented LEAP's case for ending drug prohibition by legalized regulation to more than 600 audiences around the world. He has devoted most of his adult life to his pursuit of harm reduction by working to reform law enforcement, criminal justice, and US drug policy. He retired as a detective lieutenant after a twenty-six-year career with the New

Jersey State Police—fourteen years as an undercover narcotics officer whose cases included billion dollar international narcotic trafficking organizations.

Louis Cozolino, PhD, is a Professor of Psychology at Pepperdine University (California) and an Adjunct Clinical Professor of Psychiatry at the University of California, Los Angeles. His areas of expertise include the effects of long-term stress, attachment, and brain development, and he is involved in the new field of interpersonal neurobiology. He is the author of four books: *The Neuroscience of Psychotherapy: Building and Rebuilding the Human Brain*; *The Making of a Therapist: A Practical Guide to the Inner Journey*; *The Neuroscience of Human Relationships: Attachment and the Developing Social Brain*; and *The Healthy Ageing Brain: Maintaining Attachment, Attaining Wisdom*. He presently divides his time between teaching, clinical practice, writing, and playing with his new son, Sam.

Marci Green, PhD, is a senior lecturer in sociology at the University of Wolverhampton. During the course of her career, she has specialized in the sociologies of work and inequality, labour migration, racism, gender, and labour relations, and has published on the political economy of racialization and immigration. She was drawn to the ideas of attachment theory in the mid-1990s, and has since then developed her work on attachment in conjunction with politics and sociology. In 2003, she co-edited and authored the book, *Attachment and Human Survival*.

Jennifer Leaning, PhD, teaches disaster management, human rights, and response to humanitarian crises. She has field experience in problems of disaster response and human rights (particularly in Afghanistan, Albania, Angola, Kosovo, the Middle East, former Soviet Union, Somalia, the Chad–Darfur border, and the African Great Lakes area) and has written widely on these issues. She is lead editor of *Humanitarian Crises: The Medical and Public Health Response*, published by Harvard University Press in 1999. Dr Leaning serves on a number of non-profit boards, including the Board of Directors of the American Red Cross, Massachusetts Bay Chapter, and Physicians for Human Rights. Her research and policy interests include problems of international human rights and international humanitarian law, humanitarian crises, and medical ethics in practical settings of disasters and emergencies.

Diane Levin, PhD, is Professor of Education at Wheelock College in Boston, Massachusetts. She is an internationally recognized expert on the effects that violence, media, and commercial culture are having on children. She is the author or co-author of eight books, including: *So Sexy So Soon* (in press); *The War Play Dilemma: What Every Parent and Teacher Needs to Know*; *Teaching Young Children in Violent Times: Building a Peaceable Classroom*; and *Remote Control Childhood? Combating the Hazards of Media Culture.* She is co-founder of Teachers Resisting Unhealthy Children's Entertainment (TRUCE) and Campaign for a Commercial-Free Childhood (CCFC).

Peter Marris was associated with the Institute of Community Studies, London, for seventeen years, and then the Centre for Environmental Studies, before joining the Urban Planning Programme at the University of California, Los Angeles, in 1976, where he was based until 1991. He has taught at the University of California, Berkeley, MIT, Boston University, the University of Massachusetts, Boston, Brandeis University, Makerere University, and Yale University. Peter has undertaken research on housing and local economic development, community action and loss, in both the UK and the USA, as well as in East and West Africa. His books include: *The Politics of Uncertainty: Attachment in Public and Private Life*; *Meaning and Action*; *Loss and Change*; and *Dilemmas of Social Reform* (with Martin Rein). A recent monograph, *Witnesses, Engineers and Storytellers, Using Research for Social Policy and Action*, reflects on his experience of research in the context of policy and social action.

Chris Purnell is a registered member of the Centre for Attachment-based Pychoanalytic Psychotherapy and works as a specialist adult psychotherapist in the National Health Service (UK), as well as running a small private practice. He has an interest in adult attachment generally, and particularly in the application of attachment theory in psychotherapeutic work. He has published a number of papers on this subject in several books and journals.

Katharine Shubinsky is a UK-based psychotherapist. She has worked with children, families, and adults for thirty years, initially as a social worker and then as an integrative psychotherapist (having trained at the Sherwood Psychotherapy Training Institute). She has been active in the Women's Movement and in a wide range of community campaigns for many years, and has developed a particular interest in the role of individual, family, and environmental factors in resolving childhood trauma. She currently works with adults as a psychotherapist for the National Health Service. Among her clients are refugees and asylum seekers who have experienced trauma as adults, and for whom she seeks to provide a therapeutic environment and raise public awareness of their needs.

Michelle D. Walker, MA, is a doctoral candidate in Clinical Psychology at Pepperdine University (California). For the past several years she has been training with Dr Louis Cozolino to utilize interpersonal neurobiology as a framework for conceptualizing psychopathology. Her dissertation research looks at the possible contribution of the human mirror neuron system to antisocial personality disorder.

Joan Woodward is an attachment-based psychotherapist, author, and researcher. She started her professional life as a psychiatric social worker, and was a founder member of the Birmingham Women's Counselling and Therapy Centre (UK). She now takes a particular interest in the psychological aspects of ageing. She is the author of numerous articles and books, including *Understanding Ourselves* and *The Lone Twin*.

Introduction

Human security: self and society

A bomb goes off and a village is destroyed. The bulldozers come in and a town is levelled. A government makes war and people are dispossessed. A pharmaceutical company withholds HIV drugs, and babies are orphaned. These are events that undermine human security. And this means several things.

Homes, hospitals, schools, and industries may disappear overnight, and, without them, we cannot shelter, heal, educate, or feed a population. Furthermore, one's trust in the continuity and meaning of everyday life is suspended as the networks of social life dissolve. Then, too, the loss of a parent, a child, a sibling, a spouse, a teacher, or preacher, or community leader may bring intolerable pain, and threaten one's sense of self and place.

According to the Human Security Centre, to be secure is to be free "from pervasive threats to people's rights, their safety or even their lives" (Human Security Centre, 2005, p. 1). This conception of human security, though fairly new, expresses the thinking of numerous local, national, and global groups and agencies that work to help populations in conflict and relieve the suffering when violence occurs. Their tasks are huge and their efforts courageous.

The Centre's approach to security is useful, but let me suggest that to the Centre's list—"rights, safety and life"—we add another condition. That is, freedom of threats to attachments. By attachments, we mean more than family, friends, and acquaintances (although they may be our attachment figures). Attachments are particular kinds of affectional bonds in which we invest our psychological and physical safety; they are essential to our physical and psychological health and development. By recognizing the role of attachments in human growth, we can enhance our conception of human security in two ways. First, we widen our understanding of the forms those threats might take. Second, we deepen our comprehension of the risks to security that derive from attachment traumas.

For example, we know that political violence undermines our safety, but there are other conditions that may threaten our security with equal consequence, such as the perfectly ordinary ways in which societies operate. We have in mind the organization and expectations of a workplace and labour market that separates children from care-givers; cultural values that embrace individualism and competition over mutuality and co-operation; those child-rearing conventions that bend a child's will to an adult's needs; government policies that put last the vulnerable and weak; cultures of consumption that confuse material acquisition with emotional well-being; the drives of the market that put profit before personhood; and the relations of power embedded in our social institutions (Marris, 1996). These institutional and cultural forces influence the quality of human connection and our judgements of human worth. But, as compelling as these forces can be, they may well undermine what we need in order to feel secure.

This is because those institutional arrangements and cultural systems influence our ability to make and maintain secure attachments. According to attachment theory, the foundations of secure attachments are established in infancy and early childhood when our primary care-givers are "there" for us in appropriate ways; they enable the growth of stable personalities capable of self-reliance and exploration, empathy with others, and the ability to manage disappointments and distress (Bowlby, 1999, pp. 103–125).

When our attachments are insecure or have "failed" as a result of experiences of unwanted separation from, or loss of, care-givers, inconsistent care-giving, physical and mental abuse, and disruptions or violations of other affectional bonds, a child's sense of self and relational abilities can be damaged. The trauma that results may induce depression, the drive towards self-harm, a distrust of one's ability to survive and get one's needs met, violence towards others, and an inability to parent one's own children appropriately. Thus, the routine and accepted ways of organizing social and cultural life are as much a matter of human security as is political violence.

The extraordinary and commonplace risks to security are connected in complex ways. For example, political violence can destroy those institutional arrangements that sustain social life (Apfel & Simon, 1996). In turn, this may weaken our capacity to make and sustain our attachment bonds and diminish those emotional and social resources we can mobilize in order to recover. In these circumstances, losses accumulate. It is also the case that our ability to manage the traumas of violence may depend on the quality of our early attachment experiences. Studies suggest that early attachment security helps to provide some emotional protection from the effects of later traumatic experiences.

In another way, too, the risks are intimately connected. A child's insecurity from early failed attachment could later be expressed in the harmful behaviours of the adult that child might become. A child who feels consistently powerless might become the adult who seeks power over others. If that adult then abuses a child, directs industries or armies, rules a nation, or builds bombs, they might help to reproduce those very experiences of insecurity from which they might have suffered as children. As Alice Miller argues in so much of her work, the next cycle of risk begins, as the victims of trauma in one generation create the threats to security in the next. (See, for example, Miller, 1984, 1987, 1991.)

Thus, attachment experiences matter for both the health of individuals and the quality of the human community within and across generations. It makes sense, then, to understand the threats to security in attachment terms. This is a notion of security that acknowledges the connection of private to public life, the self to society, and, as Cozolino argues, neurons to neighbourhoods to nations (see Chapter Two).

It is this conception of human security that informs this book. Through a selection of case studies, we explore the risks to human security that public life may pose.

Introducing attachment theory

> Evidence is accumulating that human beings of all ages are happi-
> est and able to deploy their talents to best advantage when they are
> confident that standing beside them is one or more trusted persons
> who will come to their aid should difficulties arise. The person
> trusted, also known as an Attachment Figure, can be considered as
> providing his or her companion with a *secure base* from which to
> operate. [Bowlby, 1999, p. 102, my emphasis]

The principles of attachment theory are presented throughout
this book, but it is useful to introduce some of the key ideas that guide
our discussion. As with any field of study, especially one that draws
on so many disciplines as does this theory, there is considerable
debate. None the less, we can identify some foundational themes.

John Bowlby, the originator of attachment theory, argued that
human beings are born biologically predisposed to attach to their
primary care-giver(s). Influenced by ethology, among other things,
Bowlby believed that human beings seek attachments as a condition of self and species survival, as do other primates. However, for
human beings, whose brains mature largely outside the womb,
cumulative experiences of attachments, unwanted separation, and
loss are especially significant for physical and psychological growth
(*ibid.*, pp. 25–43). There is nothing sentimental about this notion of
attachment: attachments entail specific experience-dependent neu-
rological and relational processes.

Over the first two years of life, infants establish a hierarchy of
attachment figures. It is these attachment figures whom an infant
recognizes as a source of security, and to whom they turn to have
their attachment needs met. Primary among these needs are to be
valued, safe, soothed, loved, and "held favourably in the mind" of
their primary care-giver(s). The better able the care-giver(s) to meet
her or his needs, the more likely the infant will feel that the care-
giver(s) will provide both a *secure haven* (a place to return for comfort and safety when fearful) and a *secure base* (the trusted point of
reference from which to explore the environment).

It is especially in times of distress that we seek proximity to our
care-giver(s); this proximity-seeking is what we call attachment
behaviour and is mobilized in all primates. However, for human

infants and children, both access to one's care-giver *and the experiences of how well their attachment needs are met* are especially significant. This is, not least, because our early attachment experiences help to shape brain development; the brain is a *social* organ that grows in relation to its attachment and wider relational environment. Furthermore, our attachment experiences (and our other affectional bonds) will influence the perceptions we hold of ourselves and our capacities to engage with others; this is because early attachment experiences help to construct the internal mental maps by which we navigate our emotional and social environments.

One of the distinctive ideas of attachment theory is that attachment bonds persist throughout life. Paraphrasing Bowlby (*ibid.*, p. 130), Woodward captures this insight when she argues that while the quality of attachments change as we mature and "are supplanted by new bonds", they will "continue to engage us in our most intense emotions" (2004, p. 8). For example,

> [t]his occurs during their formation ("falling in love"), in their maintenance (which we describe as loving), and in their loss (which we know as "grieving"). If the loss of these bonds is threatened, both anxiety and anger are aroused. Their actual loss gives rise to sorrow, but their renewal is a source of joy. [*ibid.*]

Thus, attachments matter "from cradle to grave". To need others is to be human. Unfortunately, this need is too often perceived in our cultures as a sign of immaturity and childish dependency. How confused we must feel when our ordinary desires for value and security are disparaged as inappropriate in adult life.

The early psychological and physical drive for attachment is universal. Research suggests that even in communities where care-giving is shared, infants and children, especially in times of distress, will seek out those particular attachment figures with whom they feel safe. Of course, communities will organize their attachment resources in different ways, but, however care-giving is arranged, the proximity and responsiveness of care-givers influence psychological and social development

Several decades of attachment (and neuro-scientific) research have provided us with good evidence on the importance of attachment experiences for brain development, psychological states, parenting and relational abilities, and the generational transmission of attachment patterns. Much of this research has been on the quality of intimate, one-to-one exchanges between infant and attachment figures, and the psychological and behavioural *patterns* (*styles*) these exchanges help to create. (See, for example, Ainsworth, Blehar, Waters, & Wall, 1978; Hesse & Main, 2000; Karen, 1994.)

These patterns express the ways in which we seek, and operate within, relationships, and manage the feelings of intimacy, separation, loss, and reunion. Since the late 1950s, attachment researchers, primarily in Western societies, have been developing diagnostic tools to identify attachment styles, with the earliest—observational—studies focusing on infant–mother interactions. Over recent decades, these tools have expanded and been refined to better understand infants' attachment patterns, to map styles of parenting, and to chart the attachment patterns that emerge as we mature.

Just how well these particular diagnostic tools apply across all societies is unclear, and we require much more cross-cultural research. Then, too, human beings are more complex than the tools represent. None the less, in relation to the samples—from mainly American and European families—they have generated some useful findings. One of the messages from the evidence is that there is remarkable consonance between the attachment patterns of infants and children, and the parenting styles of their primary care-givers (usually the mother). (In the early studies, infant–care-giver interactions were observed between infants and their mothers. However, subsequent research recognizes that fathers and other primary care-givers can be attachment figures. To indicate this, I shall place quotation marks around "mother" to indicate that "mothering" may be done by a range of primary care-givers.)

Furthermore, we find that attachment patterns from childhood are reasonable predictors of the kind and quality of relationships that infants and children will form throughout life. (One's cultural environment plays an important role in shaping the behaviours through which attachment styles are expressed. The evidence suggests that these behaviours tend to be gendered, so that, for example, insecure–avoidant females are more likely to be withdrawn as a result of depression, turning their pain inwards, while males are more likely turn their aggression outwards towards others.) Examples of attachment patterns and how they affect development are given below.

Securely attached. This decribes those infants whose attachment fig-
ure(s) provides a secure base, is attuned to their needs and whose
care-giving is appropriately responsive and consistent. These
infants will feel confident to explore, but will seek out attachment
figure(s) when distressed. They are able to form close friendships in
childhood and, as adults, are likely to manage intimate relationships
with reasonable confidence and flexibility (Karen, 1994, p. 443).

Insecure–avoidant. Infants whose primary caregiver(s) has been "dismissive" and often emotionally unavailable demonstrate the insecure–avoidant pattern. The infant is uncomfortable in physical
contact with "mother", and will be unresponsive to being held
(*ibid.*, p. 442). She or he is likely to become a child who finds close
friendships, and physical contact with parents, difficult. As an
adult, she or he is likely to be emotionally detached and unable to
empathize with the feelings of others. This attachment style might
indicate a predisposition to violent behaviour.

Insecure–ambivalent. These infants are those whose attachment fig-
ure(s) has been unpredictable in her responses to the infant's needs.
The infant will cry often, be "clingy and demanding, often angry
and upset by small separations . . ." (*ibid.*). She or he is preoccupied
with trying to please and get the mother's attention. She or he is
likely to become a child who will seek intimacy with, but feel hostile towards, the parents, and is also likely to find friendships hard
to sustain. As an adult, she or he will be preoccupied by feelings of
anger and hurt towards the parents and will find relationships
problematic.

Insecure–disorganized. This attachment category includes those
infants whose "mother" has been disorganized, chaotic, and frightening in her responses to baby. The infant may be fearful of the very
person in whom she or he would seek a safe haven (resulting in
fright without solution) and is likely to exhibit a "diverse arrange
of . . . odd, disorganized, disoriented, or overtly conflicted behav-
iors in the parents' presence" (Hesse & Main, 2000, p. 1099). The
infant is likely to become a child who will be inexplicably fearful
and confused, may have violent fantasies, will have problems
empathizing with others and be predisposed to disruptive and
aggressive behaviour (*ibid.*, p. 1110). As adults, their behaviour is

likely to be frightened, and frightening to others, and they are at great risk of psychopathology.

Importantly, these patterns are not exclusive—an individual can develop more than one pattern (say through experiences of attachment to more than one primary care-giver). Neither are they "fixed". That is, they can be modified over time through experiences of being valued and loved by others (lovers, family, friends, colleagues) and by therapeutic intervention. However, building a secure sense of self as we mature often entails painful struggle, and some insecure–anxious patterns (e.g., avoidant and disorganized) are more resistant to change than others.

These patterns are formed in the beginning through our most intimate interactions with our attachment figures, and become a kind of template for engagement in later relationships. As we mature, of course, we experience a variety of social connections and become more complex social selves. Thus, it is important to think about the wider social environments through which attachments are shaped and continually sought.

Attachments, social relations, and public life

Attachment theory is *relational*. In other words, it is the experiences and qualities of relationships that influence our personality development. This approach is central to attachment theory, and expresses Bowby's central conviction that the threats to psychological development are largely interactional and environmental; they are external to the individual and derive from real life experiences rather than from an infant's so-called innate drives and fantasies. So, how can we understand the ways in which our environments influence our attachment experiences?

In the first instance, the "environment" is the face-to-face relationship with our care-giver(s). It is rich with gesture, touch, smell, taste, and sound. If our care-givers are appropriately responsive to our needs, then our first experiences will form the foundations of security and trust. If our care-givers do not meet our needs, or are themselves a source of trauma, then we are likely to become psychologically disturbed and will struggle to manage our emotional distress (Gerhardt, 2005; Schore, 1994; Siegel, 1999).

As we grow, our social environment widens to include friends, peers, teachers, and workmates. Importantly, those "others" who now inhabit our relational world will also play out their own attachment patterns (secure or anxious–insecure) so that we must learn to manoeuvre—with varying success—the more complex systems of human connection.

These are the more—or less—intimate environments of people we know. But our environments are also influenced by people we will never meet, and who are themselves locked into wider "public" networks of social relations. These more impersonal relations comprise, for example, social institutions (e.g., the economy, employment, religion, health, education, welfare, and the media), government policies, structures of access to material and social resources (usually unequal), and the system of norms, values, beliefs, signs, and rituals embedded in popular culture.

An individual's experiences of, and relationships in, these networks will depend, of course, on many things, such as the expectations and behaviours of those who populate them; the rules and regulations by which they operate; the structure of rewards by which material and honorarial resources are distributed; and, not least, the value that institutions and cultures place on child-rearing and affectional bonds. This value varies within and across societies. According to Bowlby, many societies do recognize the importance of attachments throughout life, and honour the work of parenting to meet the needs of children appropriately. "Paradoxically, it has taken the world's richest societies to ignore these basic facts" (Bowlby, 1993, p. 2).

To parent requires emotional resources, but it also requires material and social support. Data on the world's richest society are revealing. The American Friends Service Committee, for example, reports a decline in government funding for health and social services over a thirty-year period up to 2004 (AFSC, 2004). These trends in the USA have been sharpened by the growing privatization of healthcare, education, prisons, and military functions (*ibid.*, p. 19), a process that deepens inequalities of access to the most basic resources on which survival and security depend.

One's material resources are not necessarily indicators of an ability to make secure attachments. However, a society that routinely exposes its members to ill health and premature death from poor healthcare provision (*ibid.*, p. 22), that leaves families hungry and homeless, and that deprives the already vulnerable of decent education, employment, sustainable wages, hope, and justice (the poor—especially people of colour—are over-represented in the prison system of the USA) is a society that jeopardizes secure attachments and emotional health. Data from the National Incidence Studies of Child Abuse and Neglect in the USA show that, since 1986, there has been a significant increase in the proportion of children both "at risk" and "endangered by" physical, sexual, and emotional abuse and neglect; the most vulnerable children are those from large families, those in single parent families, and those from families on low and very low incomes (Sedlak & Broadhurst, 1996). (The fourth NIS study is now near completion; this is a more comprehensive study in the USA, evaluating trends up until 2006. For a discussion of the research design, and other information about the current study, see: www.nis4.org/nis4.asp.)

Thus, the structures of public life may diminish (or enhance) our sense of security as we manage the muddling and often harsh demands of our institutions, economy, and culture. They also, of course, might inhibit—or enable—our ability to parent or provide security for others who need our care.

In turn, we might also carry our early attachment styles *into* public life. For example, if we have suffered attachment insecurities and they remain unresolved, our conduct towards others might be dismissive, erratic, and even violent. We might seek authority and power over others in ways that give us some sense of security, however fleeting and fragile, while diminishing the integrity (or destroying the lives) of those with whom we are connected. The racist, the sexist, the macho manager, the punitive maker of policy, and the power-driven politician, are, after all, just people with their own attachment styles. And, there might be a limit to the protection that codes of public conduct and the law provide us in the face of an individual's unresolved traumas. Indeed, these codes and laws might be made by those very people who have been insecurely attached, so that patterns of insecure behaviour can texture public life. As de Zulueta argues, the routes between personal suffering and public behaviour can be travelled in both directions, with consequences within, and across, generations (de Zulueta, 1994; see also Miller, 1987).

Most research in the field of attachment is on the experiences of attachment, separation, and loss and their developmental course and effects. In this book we widen our vision to the conditions and processes of attaching that are constrained—or enabled—by the structures of public life. Here, we look at examples of how social institutions, cultural systems, and social policies may undermine our ability to make and maintain secure attachments. We also consider the prospects for enabling change.

The spirit of this work is adventurous and reflective. It has to be, as we explore away from the more secure base of scientific and clinical findings that attachment research has accumulated. To write about the connections between the self and society, and private and public life, requires a kind of sociological and political vision that is mindful of the great varieties of human community, the many ways in which attachment networks may operate, and the complex connections that exist amongst socio-economic systems, power relations, institutional life, culture, psycho-biography and psychobiology. For the purposes of this book, however, we will limit our discussion to examples from mainly the UK and the USA.

The contributors to this book are drawn from many fields. We are, variously, clinical practitioners, researchers, social scientists, educators, political campaigners, and human rights advocates. We are based largely in the UK and the USA, although we have worked in the Caribbean, China, and Africa. Some of us are schooled in attachment theory, while others have become attuned to the issues of attachment in the course of our professional and political activity. For this book, all of us have pushed our ideas in new directions, and have done so using both the useful signposts that attachment research has provided, and the experiences we have gained through our work.

This book is divided into three parts. Part I introduces readers to the basic principles of attachment theory and their value in helping us understand why secure attachments are so important to the health of persons and communities. In this Introduction, I have suggested that risks to human security derive as much from everyday life as they do from political violence. I also argue that these risks are connected. For one thing, both create trauma from the losses, disruptions, and violations of attachments and affectional bonds. Second, one's attachment insecurities may be played out in public life, with risks to present and future generations. To create real security, then, requires recognition of the importance of attachments to human development, and the tangled relations that bind self to society.

In Chapter One, Lou Cozolino and Michelle D. Walker continue the discussion of attachment theory by anchoring its principles in neuroscience. The human brain, they argue, develops socially through interaction. It is an organ of "adaptation" that is built at the interface between experience (nurture) and genetics (nature). They introduce us to the complex processes of brain development and illuminate the extraordinary connections of neurons to neighbourhoods to nations.

Most attachment research addresses the *intimate* character of the attachment processes and effects. However, attachment theory argues that the wider social and political context in which attachments and affectional bonds are established figure significantly in the quality of our private and interpersonal development. It is to this wider context that we turn in Part II.

In some instances, the effects of public life on attachments are direct: for example, from political conflict, forced migration and dispossession, imprisonment, and economic and social policies that diminish the ties of family and community. In other instances, the impact is indirect, arising from the erosion or neglect of conditions that enable parents or other primary care-givers to be present for their children in appropriate ways, and from the failure of our institutions, cultural systems, and social policies to regard the importance of attachments and affectional bonds throughout the lifespan; examples of these would include the organization and practices of a workplace and labour market, inadequate provision for childcare and dependents, the pressures of aggressive market practices and consumer culture, child-rearing conventions, the failure of public services to provide material and emotional support for vulnerable people, and the mismanagement of communities in the aftermath of trauma

In Part II, contributors reflect upon some of the complex connections between public life and the quality of our attachments. In some respects, our choice of topics is arbitrary; there are just so many examples of the ways in which both the extraordinary and routine features of public life may put our attachments at risk. Here, we have selected indicative case studies that illuminate aspects of institutional life, culture, and social policy that undermine relational life.

Attachments are unique kinds of affectional bonds. One expression of their significance for emotional well-being is the grief we feel when attachments are broken. In Chapter Two, Peter Marris explores their importance in the context of communities that have suffered collective trauma from environmental disasters and economic change. He argues that, in these instances, the capacity to mourn loss and manage trauma depends on the recognition, by disaster agencies and policy makers, of the particularity of attachments and the role they play in sustaining for persons and communities a meaningful and continuous sense of self. And yet, welfare and economic policies, he claims, take no account of the unique nature of the attachment bond. Consequently, they often both promote loss and undermine support for recovery.

Work is an essential life activity on which economies and social systems depend. It also provides the material and social resources we need for our economic survival, self esteem and engagement in society. But, the needs of "the system" might weaken our capacity to feel secure in our selves and provide security for others. In Chapter Three, I consider three examples of working patterns in late capitalist society, and argue that the intensification of work pressures and the sacrifices these entail can heighten our need for attachments and affectional bonds while depriving us of the very opportunities we need to establish and maintain them.

One of the casualties of labour migration is unwanted separation and loss. In Chapter Four, Elaine Arnold considers the problems faced by Afro-Caribbean immigrants and their families who came to work in the United Kingdom in the mid twentieth century. She argues that the suffering they endured from disrupted and broken attachments was deepened by the failure of national and local government bodies to appreciate the importance of familial and community bonds in the process of migration, settlement, and reunion. She also argues that the emotional costs of the migration experience and the socio-political environment into which migrants came have influenced the psychological health of subsequent generations.

The theme of migration continues in Chapter Five, which highlights the experiences of people who have lost their secure base through *forced* separation from families, loved ones, and communities, and have sought asylum in the UK. Chris Purnell and Kath Shubinsky describe their experiences of working therapeutically with refugees and asylum seekers to help them overcome their trauma, and highlight some ways in which the media and social policies have compounded their sense of displacement and loss.

In Chapter Six, Diane Levin focuses on the changes in children's emotional and relational skills that result from the pressures of the media and the aggressive market practices of contemporary consumer cultures. She argues that, with the deregulation of the media in the 1980s in the USA, there has developed among children a growing compassion deficit disorder and a weakening ability to solve problems in relationally productive ways. She also argues that parents are increasingly confused about how best to understand and meet the consuming passions of their children.

What makes for a "just" society? One answer could be the manner in which the state safeguards the rights of its citizens and provides the means of restitution when those rights are breached. In Chapter Seven, Jack Cole explores the contradictions and human costs of the criminal justice system in the USA that have emerged from the government's "war on drugs". He argues that the war on drugs is, in truth, a war on people, and that this policy pursued in the name of justice has destroyed families and communities. In so doing, this "war" has undermined human security and contributes to those very problems that it claims to resolve.

We are social beings, and our social selves, skills, aspirations, goals, and behaviour are shaped by the cultural systems and institutional arrangements in which our lives are enmeshed. These structures of public life are powerful, but we often take them for granted as simply "how things are"—until, of course, they obstruct our efforts to meet our social and emotional needs. At those moments, their power is exposed, and then we may feel vulnerable and helpless in our efforts to direct our lives. However, since society is, ultimately, of human making, it is possible to do things differently. In Part III, we consider strategies for enabling change so that our culture, social policies, and institutional practices can come to embrace the principle that attachments and affectional bonds matter for human security.

In Chapter Eight, Jennifer Leaning returns us to the concept of human security, and invites us to consider its importance in guiding the approach that international bodies take to populations emerging from war, oppression, or major disaster. The concept of human security employed by Leaning has three components: a sense of home, a link to community, and a positive sense of future possibilities. Her approach, therefore, challenges the emphasis by governments on arms accumulation and political brokerage, and moves towards a focus on the psycho-social dynamics of individuals and communities caught in a continuum of suffering (through profound loss, dislocation, and the experience of atrocity). Using this model of human security, Leaning demonstrates its real theoretical and policy applications for populations in pre-conflict, conflict, and post-conflict environments. She concludes that while every war is different, "each yields, to those who look for it, a recognizable pattern of human attachment and loss". Policies on human security, therefore, must embrace what opportunities arise in conflict situations, to enhance attachment and mitigate loss.

One of the obstacles to enabling change is the powerful resistance that is generated by those with strong interests in maintaining the status quo, even when, in so doing, they place our attachments and affectional bonds at risk. In Chapter Nine, Woodward considers a variety of resistances to change, and shares her experiences as a psychotherapist and community activist exploring ways of overcoming them. She argues that one source of resistance to valuing attachments resides in the principle that lies at their heart, which is love; "love is mutual and horizontal, whereas power structures are hierarchical and vertical", and for this reason, love is considered subversive. Another powerful source of resistance to change comes from the psychological defences that those in power might mobilize to repress the knowledge of their own attachment history and the effect this has had upon them. To acknowledge the attachment needs of others is to confront oneself. Thus, to enable change requires an understanding not only of the culture and practices that are entrenched in the structures of public life, but also of the psychological barriers among individuals who feel threatened by them

However powerful are the social forces within our institutions and popular culture that may inhibit our efforts to make and maintain secure attachments, it is necessary to challenge them. Marris reminds us of the reasons why:

> The qualities of good social relationships and good experiences of attachment are essentially the same: predictability, responsiveness, intelligibility, supportiveness, reciprocity of commitment. To

achieve this, we have to struggle constantly against the tendency of the powerful to subordinate and marginalize others in the interest of their own greater security. The worse we fail, the more wide-spread insecurity becomes and the greater the temptation to rescue our own command of circumstances at the expense of others. . . . We need to institute a style of governing our relationships with each other, which takes as its first principles reciprocity of commit-ment, predictability, and respect for the unique structure of mean-ing and attachment which makes life worthwhile for each of us. It is a radically more collaborative and democratic style of govern-ment than any we have experienced . . . [S]uch a style of creating and reproducing social relationships responds to our deepest and most universal need to create a world in which we dare become attached. [Marris, 1991, p. 89]

Those of us who have contributed to this book are conscious of the risks to human security that reside in the structures of public life. Yet, we are optimistic. There is a growing interest in the prin-ciples and practical uses of attachment theory for individuals and groups. Furthermore, we are part of an international body of researchers, practitioners, and activists who recognize the impor-tance of attachments for the quality of human life. In the enterprise of this book, we invite our readers to reflect on those risks, and to seek ways that will make life secure.

Marci Green
October 2008

References

Ainsworth, M., Blehar, M., Waters, E., & Wall, S. (1978). *Patterns of Attachment: Assessed in the Strange Situation and at Home*. Hillsdale, NJ: Erlbaum.

American Friends Service Committee (AFSC) (2004). *Putting Dignity and Rights at the Heart of the Global Economy: A Quaker Perspective*. Philadelphia, PA: AFSC. www.afsc.org/resources/items/putting-dignity-right-global-perspective.htm (accessed 12 April 2007).

Apfel, R. J., & Simon, B. (1996). *Minefields in Their Hearts: The Mental Health of Children in War and Communal Violence*. New Haven, CT: Yale University Press.

Bowlby, J. (1993). *A Secure Base: Clinical Applications of Attachment Theory*. London: Routledge.

Bowlby, J. (1999). *The Making and Breaking of Affectional Bonds*. London: Routledge.

de Zulueta, F. (1993). *From Pain to Violence: The Roots of Human Destructiveness*. London: Whurr.

Gerhardt, S. (2005). *Why Love Matters: How Affection Shapes a Baby's Brain*. London: Routledge.

Hesse, E., & Main, M. (2000). Disorganized infant, child and adult attachment: collapse in behavioral and attentional strategies. *Journal of the American Psychoanalytic Association*, *48*(4): 1097–1127.

Human Security Centre (2005). *The Human Security Report 2005*. Accessed 30 March 2007.

Iraq Analysis Group (2007). The rising costs of the Iraq war. www.iraq-analysis.org/publications/235 Accessed 22 March 2007.

Karen, R. (1994). *Becoming Attached*. New York: Warner.

Marris, P. (1991). The social construction of uncertainty. In: C. M. Parkes, J. Stevenson-Hinde, & P. Marris (Eds.), *Attachment Across the Life Cycle* (pp. 77–92). London: Routledge.

Marris, P. (1996) *The Politics of Uncertainty: Attachment in Public and Private Life*. London: Routledge.

Miller, A. (1984). *Thou Shalt Not Be Aware: Society's Betrayal of the Child*. New York: Meridien/New American Library

Miller, A. (1987). *For Your Own Good: Hidden Cruelty In Child-Rearing and the Roots of Violence*. Great Britain: Virago.

Miller, A. (1991). *Banished Knowledge: Facing Childhood Injuries*. New York: Anchor.

Sedlak, A. J., & Broadhurst, D. D. (1996). *Third National Incidence Study of Child Abuse and Neglect* (1996). NIS-3: US Department of Health and Human Services. See: Child welfare information gateway www.childwelfare.gov/systemwide/statistics/nis.cfm (accessed 27 June 2007).

Schore, A. N. (1994). *Affect Regulation and the Origin of the Self: The Neurobiology of Emotional Development*. Hillsdale, NJ: Ehrlbaum.

Siegel, D. J. (1999). *The Developing Mind*. New York: Guilford.

Woodward, J. (2004). Introduction to attachment theory. In: M. Green & M. Scholes (Eds.), *Attachment and Human Survival*. London: Karnac.

PART I

THE BASIC PRINCIPLES OF ATTACHMENT THEORY

CHAPTER ONE

The social construction of the human brain

Lou Cozolino and Michelle D. Walker

A fundamental characteristic of the biological sciences is to study individual organs and organisms rather than viewing them in the context of living systems and evolving communities. This bias has led us to think of the brain as an individual organ and to search for technical answers about human behaviour instead of those that arise within the lived experience of human interactions. While we have learned a great deal from the theories and methods of this type of scientific exploration, our gains have not been without costs.

A tragic example comes from the recent past in the treatment of children in orphanages. In response to high death rates assumed to be the result of infectious disease, physicians ordered that their handling be kept to a minimum and that they be isolated from one another. Despite these changes, institutionalized children continued to die at such alarming rates that death certificates were signed along with admission forms to save time (Blum, 2002). The work of Rene Spitz and John Bowlby about the importance of human contact and sustained bonding resulted in these children being assigned specific care-takers. Staff members were now encouraged to hold and play with the children and to allow them to play with one another. After these changes were instituted, mortality rates in orphanages began to decline. A lack of contact, attachment, and bonding proved more fatal than microbes.

All living systems—from neurons, to brains, to individual human beings—depend on interactions with others of their kind (Schore, 1994). From conception, each human brain is dependent on the scaffolding of care-takers and loved ones for its survival, growth, and well-being. During every moment of our lives, we affect and are affected by the biology and behaviours of those around us. Thus, to write the story of the social brain, we must begin with the thought *there are no single brains*.

We begin with what we know: the brain is a social organ, built at the interface between experience and genetics, where nature and nurture become one. Genes begin by serving as a template to organize the general structure of the brain and trigger sensitive periods of development. Later, through a process called transcription, genes orchestrate the ongoing translation of experience into neural material as the brain adapts to its particular environment. Through the biochemical alchemy of template and transcription genetics, experience becomes flesh, love takes material form, and culture is transmitted from one generation to the next (Cozolino, 2006).

Compared to other animals, humans are born extremely immature. Parents have to be very adept care-takers and babies need to come equipped with an array of reflexes designed to help them attach to their parents and communicate their needs to them. The shaping of the brain occurs within the interlocking system of children, care-takers, and the community at large. In building a brain, the ever-expanding concentric circles of parents, family, community, and culture interact and interpenetrate one another in shaping each child's nervous system. The very prematurity of the brain allows it to be maximally influenced by its particular social and physical environment. The child has to learn and adapt to an ever-changing stream of social information and constellation of relationships. This process of experience-dependent learning via transcription genetics is the process by which each generation builds the brains of their children (Siegel, 1999).

We begin life with the task of getting to know our mothers and those around us. Attuning to the smells, sights, and sounds of familiar others, we gradually learn to feel safe in their presence.

Our mothers, fathers, grandparents, and other caretakers shape our brains during the dance of interacting instincts. Certainly, babies are driven by internal forces to orientate towards, approach, touch, and interact with others. So, too, are their care-givers. For humans, other people are our primary environment.

As primates have evolved, our brains have grown increasingly larger. Larger brains have led to longer periods of childhood and juvenile dependency, as well as more complex social structures. Being a member of a complex society requires a brain that is born ready to learn a vast amount of social information that takes many years to master. The social brain systems involved in attaching and communicating with those around us are all built by, and dependent upon, experience. While we are born with many bonding reflexes, the ability to form healthy relationships must be learnt. Children have to be exposed to social interactions and taught how to be a healthy and functional member of the group. Through smell, touch, and eye contact and later via reciprocal interactions, play, and language, we become social animals by linking together across the social synapse.

The fact that the brain is such a highly specialized social organ of adaptation is both good news and bad news. The good news is that if unexpected challenges emerge, our brains have a greater chance to adapt and survive. When good-enough parental nurturing combines with good-enough genetic programming, our brains are shaped in ways that benefit us throughout life. However, the bad news is that we are just as capable of adapting to *unhealthy* environments and *pathological* care-takers. The resulting adaptations may help us survive traumatic childhoods, but may impede healthy development later in life (Cozolino, 2002). Our parents are the primary environment to which our young brains adapt and their unconscious minds are our first reality. The prejudices, strife, community violence, and deprivation that touch so many young lives also become woven into the neural fabric of each child's brain.

In the face of inadequate parental and social resources, a child's brain is often shaped in ways that do not support his long term survival, as the parent is communicating to the child that he is less fit. Non-loving behaviour signals the child's brain to develop as if the world is a dangerous place: do not explore, do not discover, do not take chances. When children are traumatized, abused, or neglected, they are being given the message that they are not among the chosen. They grow to have thoughts, states of mind, emotions, and immunological functioning that are inconsistent with well-being, successful procreation, and long-term survival. Despite the old adage suggesting that stress and deprivation build character, the truth appears to be that what does not kill us makes us *weaker*.

It is vital that we are protected from overwhelming stress during childhood because early interactions are actually building the brain and impacting the way it will function for a lifetime. These experience-dependent neural circuits are sculpted and become organized by the child's interaction with care-takers. While it is important to maximize the quality of early experience, there is considerable room for later healing and recovery. Social brain networks do retain varying degrees of plasticity throughout life. We rely on this plasticity in education and psychotherapy for new social, emotional, and cognitive learning. In addition, when we are nurturing our children, we not only build their brains, but build our own as well. Playing with a child triggers neural plasticity and neurogenesis in both brains, so in effect, we need children almost as much as they need us. I suspect that helping others, in all forms, has similar effects.

Survival of the nurtured

When I think of Darwin's survival of the fittest, I picture body builders, Alpha male gorillas, or lions stalking their ultimately doomed prey—all of the usual misconceptions about the process of evolution. But what does it mean to be the "fittest" in our modern society? Certainly, it is not the romantic notion of the noble savage. The instincts to run fast, fight others, and catch our own food have been channelled into hobbies and sports. Remember, survival of the fittest is entirely dependent on the environment to which the organism needs to adapt.

In contemporary society, the freeway is our savannah, the information superhighway our Galapagos. The real challenges are multi-tasking, balancing the demands of work and family, information management, and coping with stress. We need to maintain perspective, pick our battles carefully, and remain mindful of ourselves in the midst of countless competing demands. What prepares us best for these abilities? In some ways, it is the same thing that prepared our ancient ancestors to survive in their world—early nurturance, which plays a vital role in the development and integration of the diverse systems within our brains. Optimal sculpting of the pre-frontal cortex through healthy early relationships allows us to think well of ourselves, trust others, regulate our emotions, maintain positive expectations, and utilize our intellectual and emotional intelligence in moment-to-moment problem solving.

Maternal and paternal instincts—in fact, all care-taking behaviours—are acts of nurturance that have evolved to become more important than one's personal survival. It is my belief that the survival of our children's genes is such a powerful evolutionary mandate that most of us appear very willing to sacrifice our well-being and our lives for our children. Achieving such an altruistic state depends upon the successful inhibition of selfish, competitive, and aggressive impulses. However, in most instances, we are able to balance our own needs with those of our children; this state maximizes the likely survival of both parents and children. (Acts of nurturance or nurturing behaviours would, to my understanding, be motivated by the biochemistry of bonding and attachment that is genetically programmed, which would make it instinctual *vs.* learnt behaviour.) We can now add a corollary from attachment theory to Darwin's survival of the fittest: *those who are nurtured best, survive best.*

From neurons to neighbourhoods

Why do humans have such complex relationships, maternal instincts, friendships, family, and society? Why not be like a reptile that digs a hole, lays some eggs, and moves on? The newborns of some species even have to flee from their parents to avoid being eaten! Wouldn't life be easier without gossip, grudges, and in-laws? Perhaps not. Mother Nature loves to combine simple structures into more complex forms (Bonner, 1988). Bacteria, ants, and gazelles seem drawn together into interdependent systems. These colonies, armies, and herds of individuals are presumably better able to improve their fitness, and, hence, the chances of survival. If we are to utilize evolution as an organizing principle, we may assume that the social brain has been shaped by natural selection because inter-personal experiences enhance our fitness. Our best guess is that larger and more complex brains allow for a greater variety of responses in and across diverse environments (Mesulam, 1998).

Thus, it appears that larger, more complex, and more experi-ence-dependent brains allow for increasingly adaptive responses to environmental challenges. To accomplish this goal, evolution selected for bonding, attachment, and care-taking to provide the necessary scaffolding for the prolonged extra-uterine development required to build such complex social brains. This "socialization" of the brain also laid the foundation for increasingly sophisticated forms of communication, the emergence of spoken and written language, and the birth of culture (Dunbar, 1996). The idea of "culture" relates directly to the interconnectedness of humans in society. By thinking about culture, we begin to look at the idea of group instead of just the individual, and can focus in on shared elements between members of that group, such as their history, ways of living and being, and even stories passed on through generations. The evolution of culture, in turn, allows for higher levels of biological, behavioural, and technological complexity that emerges not simply within select individuals, but through the group as a whole.

Just as Mother Nature seems to bring individual organisms together in interrelated groups, it also appears that she likes to hold on to certain strategies for supporting their connection. If we zoom into the inner workings of the brain, we discover countless neurons that combine with other neurons to form nuclei or clusters of neurons that come together to perform some specific function. These nuclei are connected by fibre systems to each other, allowing them to form functional systems. Functional systems then become more sophisticated and complex and later can combine with one another. All of these neurons, nuclei, and neural networks stimu-late and interact with one another, keeping each other vital and alive.

Individual neurons are separated by synapses, or small gaps. These synapses are by no means empty spaces; rather, they are inhabited by a variety of chemical substances engaging in complex interactions that result in synaptic transmission. It is this synaptic transmission that stimulates each neuron to survive, to grow, and to be sculpted by experience. In fact, the activity within synapses is just as important as what takes place within the neurons themselves. Over vast expanses of evolutionary time, neural or synaptic transmission has grown ever more intricate to meet the needs of an increasingly complex brain.

When it comes down to it, does not communication between people, as complex as it is, consist of the same basic building blocks? When we smile, wave, and say hello, these behaviours are sent through the space between us via sight and sound. These electrical and mechanical messages are first received by our senses and then converted into electrochemical signals within our nervous systems that are then delivered to our brains. These internal signals generate chemical changes, electrical activation, and new behaviours that, in turn, transmit messages back across the social synapse. The social synapse is the space between us. It is also the medium through which we are linked together into larger organisms such as families, tribes, societies, and the human species as a whole.

If you can accept the metaphor of a social synapse, let us take it one step further. Neurons have three sequential levels of information exchange that are called first, second, and third messenger systems. They are (1) the communication across the synapse, that (2) changes the internal biochemistry of the cell, that (3) activates the genetic codes and protein synthesis to change cellular structure. Through these three messenger systems, neurons are stimulated to fire, grow, and interconnect with each other in an experience-dependent manner. Put another way, it is the firing patterns of neurons, based on environmental stimulation, that actually shape the neural circuitry of the brain. Through these three systems, our brains are shaped by experience and become a living reflection of our learning histories.

Zooming out from the brain to the level of individuals in relationships, could these three levels of information exchange be at work? In other words, when we interact, could we also be impacting each other's internal biological state and influencing the long-term construction of each other's brains? I believe the answer is yes. In fact, the emerging parallels among neurons within neural networks and individuals embedded in the social world may help us to bridge the social and neurosciences and provide a means of integrating clinical and research endeavours in science, public policy, and mental health.

The three messenger systems in humans

So how exactly does this apply to people? In what way could this mechanism of growth, connection, and complexity be occurring amid social interaction? While neurons appear limited to chemical communication, humans have also developed senses that can detect and analyse mechanical vibrations and pressure through our ears and skin, as well as a complex visual system designed to receive and process patterns within waves of light. Our sense of smell is a direct descendent of chemical transmission between neurons. But our four other senses of sight, hearing, taste, and touch also receive and send constant messages across the social synapse. This multiplicity of sensory channels not only allows for the independent processing of these channels, but provides for increased complexity through every kind of combination.

Consider a typical interaction while putting a child to bed. We might talk about the day and read her a story while lying next to her rubbing her back. We share smells and sounds, perhaps listening to a favourite song, push her hair out of her eyes, kiss her cheek, and tell her to "sleep tight" after talking about plans for tomorrow. All of these experiences stimulate and organize networks of the social brain. As experts in the reception and analysis of social information, our brains and bodies are primed to monitor and react to those around us. The multiple means of social communication combined with these receiving systems are analogous to the first messenger system present at a neuronal level.

The second messenger system in humans commences with the activation of social brain networks via these multiple streams of social information. Social brain systems include those that regulate proximity, fear, attachment, and social motivation and are all linked to bodily homeostasis. There are also networks that process social information, such as eye contact and facial recognition, as well as trigger imitation, interpersonal resonance, and empathy. Akin to the second messenger system in neurons, these systems support energy supply and stimulate cell growth while regulating metabolism, stress, and immunological functioning.

The first two messenger systems we have just reviewed allow for social interactions to sculpt our brains. Positive social interactions result in increased metabolic activity, mRNA synthesis, and neural growth. In other words, relationships create an internal biological environment supportive of sustained neural plasticity, exploration, and secure attachment. Ultimately, we now know that our interactions with others, in particular those that occur in early intimate relationships, significantly impact brain structure and long-term functioning—the third messenger system.

However much we focus on and learn from these internal biological processes, it is helpful to always remember that neurons are embedded within our brains, our brains embedded within our bodies, and our bodies embedded within society. Stimulated by relationships within our social worlds, millions of changes within and between neurons combine to create our emotions, personalities, and the quality of our day-to-day lives. Through the three messenger systems, others are able to activate our senses, regulate our brains and bodies, and change the shape of our neuronal structures.

Secure attachment

Human beings get attached to tattered sweaters, old cars, and reclining chairs that have taken just the right shape. These beloved objects make the world more familiar, comfortable, and just a little more safe. We also grow attached to our pets, are comforted by their presence, and grieve their loss. But beyond sweaters and pets, there is the even more significant physical depth and emotional power of our attachments to each other. We all know what attachment feels like—how we miss those we love, worry about their well-being, and how good it feels to see them after a long separation. But what exactly is attachment, and why does it exist?

The second part of that question is the easier one to answer. Attachment exists because, at least for primates like ourselves, being connected with one another has proved to be a survival advantage. Like many other living beings, we have evolved to come together in larger and larger organizations (families, tribes, villages, etc.) to stay safe and enhance survival. But the definition of attachment is a little more complicated. Fundamentally, the concept *attachment* refers to a set of thoughts, feelings, and biological processes that are involved in bonding. And while bonding with your children, spouse, extended family, and close friends are all somewhat different, they all utilize similar biochemical processes. These chemicals make us feel good when we are together and lonely and discouraged when we are apart.

Let us focus for a moment on the development of attachment schema in young children. Attachment schema are implicit memories of past relationship experiences that create perceptions of what we can expect from other people. From birth, newborns possess well-developed brain structures and neural networks that activate fear. However, it takes years to develop the neural systems involved in regulating fear. During our early years, we depend on our parents to provide the emotional regulation and fear attenuation that we are unable to provide for ourselves. For the young child, attachment is their primary means of emotional regulation.

Because very young children cannot tell us what they are thinking, we have to infer their states of mind from their behaviours. Attachment schemas in young children are measured by observing children's reactions to stressful situations and how they use their parents to regulate fear. Securely attached children go to their parents, interact with them for a while, and then resume exploration and play. Insecurely attached children will avoid their parents, become overly clingy, or engage in odd behaviour in their presence, such as spinning, hitting their heads, or falling to the ground. From these behaviours, we infer whether children have been able to derive comfort from their care-takers when they have been under stress. The belief is that these behaviours reflect underlying neurobiological processes that have been shaped by their relationship experiences. In other words, their attachment behaviours reflect the transduction of interpersonal experience into biological structure and implicit memory.

Early relationships guide the building of multiple structures and neural networks that are involved in attachment, emotional regulation, self-awareness, and empathy. Secure attachments build the brain in ways that optimize network integration, autonomic arousal, and positive coping responses. Securely attached children use other people successfully to modulate their stress and do not produce a stress hormone response when attachment figures are available. On the other hand, those with insecure attachment schema do show stress reactions in the same situations. Thus, the social behaviour of insecurely attached individuals is better described as a measure of distress and arousal rather than a positive form of coping. These children might present interpersonally and clinically as depressed, withdrawn, or unmotivated.

Another way of thinking about attachment schemas are as implicit memories that are known without being thought. They are stored in the structures of the social brain as predictions of the behaviours of others, creating expectations about the people we meet, and unconsciously guiding our reactions to them. Early attachment schemas persist into adulthood, influencing the choice of partners and the quality of our relationships. Their impact goes beyond the ability to shape our relationships; they also influence our emotional life, immunological functioning, and our experience of self.

Stephan: coming home

As a therapist, I have come to believe that *it is the power of being with others that shapes our brains.* An example of this circumstance would be eight-year-old Stephan. He was brought to the clinic by his adoptive parents, Paul and Susan, who wanted to know whether Stephan's early emotional development was negatively affecting his current intellectual functioning. They had adopted Stephan two years ago from an orphanage in Romania, and understood that he had experienced some degree of emotional deprivation during his early years.

Paul and Susan's phone calls and letters to the Romanian orphanage did not prepare them for the subtly disturbing conditions they found upon their arrival. They were greeted at the door by a kindly nurse and an uncanny silence. Before taking a tour of the building, they were asked to interact with the children as little as possible. As they walked past sterile rooms containing rows of cribs and small beds, they saw little of what we might think of as healthy childhood behaviour. At the far end of the building was a playroom where the children were brought for short periods each day while their rooms were being cleaned and disinfected. Here they sat, looking at books, or handling toys while ultimately ignoring one another.

The couple looked into the face of each child, searching for a spark of interest, anything to help them make a choice. They eventually spotted Stephan. Both Paul and Susan took a liking to him right away. "It was something about the way he looked at us," they said. Little Stephan also shared their skin colouring and had thick dark hair like Paul. To the best of anyone's knowledge, Stephan had come to the orphanage soon after birth, left there by a family that could not afford to raise him. Stephan was behind in his language development, but generally at the same level as other children his age at the orphanage. He seemed to have a special talent for drawing and some of his works had been pinned up in the nurses' office.

Paul and Susan described Stephan's behaviour at home as listless and withdrawn. At school, his teachers reported that he tended to shy away from group activities. In fact, the general level of elementary school chaos appeared to unnerve him. His parents realized that these interpersonal behaviours were probably the result of his early deprivation but had no idea how to help Stephan grow up to be a healthy and well-adjusted person.

When they brought him in to see me at the clinic, Stephan spoke fluent English and had only a slight accent that his parents said made him special in a positive way to the other children at school. The new testing done at the clinic revealed that Stephan's intellectual development had essentially caught up with his eight-year-old American classmates. Paul and Susan were certainly happy to hear the good news and were gratified that the clinic staff recognized the value of all their dedication and hard work.

Stephan's social deprivation came at a time when the brain relies on human contact and attuned relationships to help build circuitry dedicated to fear and emotional regulation. These neural networks help in later years to filter and modulate stimulation that allows us to better navigate our complex social worlds. At the same time, interactions build networks dedicated to eye contact, face recognition, knowing how to interpret facial expressions, and monitoring the infinite number of cues that we receive from those around us; there is, here, a constant flow of information and stimulation across the social synapse.

When Stephan was left alone with me, his strikingly dark eyes seemed listless and withdrawn. He responded to questions with short answers and avoided engaging with me by occupying himself with toys and books. Over the course of a few weeks, the clinic staff listened, watched, and interacted with Stephan and his family. There were a number of things we wanted to try to help Stephan feel more comfortable around others, increase his eye contact, and ease him into interactive play. We thought he might benefit from learning some coping strategies for dealing with the sensory overload of school, parties, and other social events where there were many people and lots of stimulation. But he needed something safer and more predictable than a group of rambunctious eight-year-olds.

During one of our sessions in the courtyard, I noticed that a dog caught his attention. Later in the session he drew a dog similar to the one that had happened by. I asked his parents if Stephan had ever had a dog. They said they once took him to find a puppy, but when they started jumping and licking and doing all the things puppies do, Stephan became afraid and ran away. Paul and Susan assumed that they had made a mistake, but I suggested they try again with a well-socialized older dog.

Soon thereafter, they found Max, a dog who had been orphaned by the death of his elderly owner. He was calm, gentle, well past puppyhood, and accustomed to sitting quietly. So here were Stephan and Max, two beings who had been orphaned. Perhaps, with some luck, they might understand and connect with one another. When Max was brought home, Stephan's eyes widened. He seemed anxious and confused about what to do. Fortunately, Max had no such problems. He walked slowly over to Stephan, sat next to him, and put his head gently under Stephan's hand. "It was as if Max knew exactly what to do," his parents told me. That night, as Paul and Susan listened at Stephan's door, they heard him teaching Max the names of his friends, the teachers he liked best, and the neighbours to avoid if you wanted to stay out of trouble. "I wasn't born here either," Stephan told Max, "but you don't have to worry because Mum and Dad won't make you go away."

Max and Stephan were inseparable, and there is nothing like a big friendly dog to attract other children. Max not only soothed

Stephan's fears, but created a bridge with the world around him. With Max's help Stephan slowly crossed that bridge, growing brave enough to begin to look the world in the eye. When we think of Stephan's experience with his parents and the quality and nature of their attachments, we naturally wonder how all of these experiences will shape Stephan's brain. How will biochemical changes affect his ability to handle stress and the strength of his immune system? How will his implicit memories affect his ability to bond with and attach to others as he grows into adulthood?

All of our brains rely on a protected and gradual introduction to the world. We depend on the attention and nurturance of our caretakers as they depend on those who surround them for support and loving care. I am hopeful about Stephan's future, based on the care and concern I could see being provided by his new mum and dad.

Interwoven hearts

I felt connected to Stephan from the moment I first saw him. Besides all the instinctual appeal of an adorable eight-year-old, I could see the pain and fear in Stephan's face. Seeing his discomfort only added to my urge to approach, engage with, and soothe him. My unconscious memories of being a frightened and confused child may have resonated in a way that made my desire to take care of him a way of soothing myself (Cozolino, 2004). By communicating through actions, gestures, touch, sounds, and words, we gradually bridged the social synapse, soothing and perhaps healing some of the emotional pain within each of us.

This complex, magical, and sometimes scary phenomenon we call human relationships is all around us. We know how it feels to bond and attach, we are beginning to understand the underlying neurobiology of these complex processes, and we can look out into the world and see the importance of addressing these issues in everyday human experience. How the connections occur, what impact they have on us, and how relationships change the architecture and functioning of the brain are all essential questions of interpersonal neurobiology. Far from detaching ourselves from felt experience, as is routinely accepted as the operative mode of science, our work *requires* the inclusion of our experience. Translating our findings into psychotherapy, parenting, education, and public policy lies ahead of us.

There is considerable evidence supporting the profound impact of early nurturance on the shaping of the social brain. As an organ of adaptation, the brain can adapt to any environment, including those not conducive to health and positive social functioning. When our childhood relationships are frightening, abusive, or non-existent, our brains dutifully adapt to the realities of our unfortunate situations. Because the core of the social brain is also the hub of our fear circuitry, negative early experiences can result in social relationships that act as a stimulus cue for troubling memories. However, there is reason to believe that these circuits retain experience-dependent plasticity throughout life, especially in close relationships.

Research suggests that, in the transition from dating to marriage, there is a broad tendency for partners with insecure and disorganized attachment to develop increasingly secure patterns. This retained plasticity in attachment circuitry makes sense from an evolutionary perspective, given the naturally occurring changes in our social situations over time. For many of us, adult relationships give us a second, third, and fourth chance at shaping our attachment circuitry and living a happy and satisfying life. Half a century ago, these insights led systems theorists to shift the focus of psychotherapy from the individual patient to the family unit. A systemic approach posits that the symptoms of the identified patient are, in fact, a by-product of the family's struggle for anxiety reduction and homeostasis. But is the family the best frame of reference from which to understand human experience? Should we zoom even further out? After all, families are embedded within communities, and communities embedded within nations.

The implications of the social construction of the human brain are vast. They extend from the sweet moments of silent mutual gaze between mother and infant to communication and co-operation between nations. My hope is that as the evidence of the impact of early experience mounts, it will become clear that we need to invest in our children and our children's children even before they are born. I hope that we will come to realize that multi-generation integration serves to benefit elders and children alike. The quality of our connections with one another has a profound impact on our health, longevity, and immunological functioning. Presumably, we stand to learn a great deal from zooming in *and* out, from neurons to neighbourhoods to nations. This way, we may gain a deeper understanding of the interwoven tapestry of biological, psychological, and social processes that make up human life.

References

Blum, D. (2002). *Love at Goon Park*. Cambridge: Perseus.

Bonner, J. T. (1988).*The Evolution of Complexity by Means of Natural Selection*. Princeton, NJ: Princeton University Press.

Cozolino, L. J. (2002). *The Neuroscience of Psychotherapy: Building and Rebuilding the Human Brain*. New York: W. W. Norton.

Cozolino, L. J. (2004). *The Making of a Therapist: A Practical Guide for the Inner Journey*. New York: W. W. Norton.

Cozolino, L. J. (2006). *The Neuroscience of Human Relationships: Attachment and the Developing Social Brain*. New York: W. W. Norton.

Dunbar, R. I. (1996). *Grooming ,Gossip, and the Evolution of Language*. Cambridge: Harvard University Press.

Mesulam, M. M. (1998). From sensation to cognition. *Brain*, *121*: 1013–1052.

Schore, A. N. (1994). *Affect Regulation and the Origin of the Self: The Neurobiology of Emotional Development*. Hillsdale, NJ: Erlbaum.

Siegel, D. J. (1999). *Developing Mind: Toward a Neurobiology of Interpersonal Experience*. New York: Guilford.

PART II

THE CONNECTIONS BETWEEN
PUBLIC LIFE AND
PERSONAL ATTACHMENT

CHAPTER TWO

Attachment and loss of community

Peter Marris

W hy do we grieve for the loss of an attachment, Freud asked in his pioneering essay "Mourning and melancholia" (Freud, 1917e). Grief is painful and conflicted, provoking impulses of nostalgia and escape that bring no lasting comfort to the present. Its moods of apathy and despair, of anger and social withdrawal, can seem pathological. It appeared, Freud thought, to fulfil no useful mental function. Why did the libido not attach itself promptly to a new object?

In the past fifty years, the work of John Bowlby, Colin Murray Parkes, Robert Weiss, and many others has shown that grieving, far from being pathological, is an essential process of healing (Bowlby, 1973; Parkes, 1975; Parkes & Weiss, 1983). The failure to grieve, rather, leaves the bereaved at risk of emotional breakdown. The loss of a crucial attachment is not simply the loss of a relationship, but the loss of all the assumptions and everyday habits that depended on it. This is especially true when the loss is untimely and unforeseen. "The bottom fell out of my world," as one young widow once told me. The whole structure of meaning that sustained her life had fallen apart. Grieving is the struggle to repair that structure, and the way someone accomplishes it is unique, because the attachment itself (and, hence, the feelings, assumptions, purposes, and habits which have been organized around it) is unique.

Bowlby speculated that the attachment bond between mother and child had evolved as a survival trait in the prehistoric human environment (Bowlby, 1969, pp. 179–180). Whatever its origin, the specificity of attachment is crucial to understanding the meanings that stem from it. We love this mother, this father, this man or woman, and every attempt to substitute more generalized ideals of brother or sisterhood has stumbled over this stubborn particularity of our attachments. Nor can a new attachment replace one that has been lost, because it cannot have the same meaning. Recovery from bereavement depends instead upon rescuing the essential meaning of the lost attachment from the trauma and despair of loss, while reinterpreting it to meet the altered circumstances of life. We do not simply mourn a lost attachment until the pain fades away. We have to come to terms with the loss, finding a way to incorporate some-one we loved very much, who is no longer present to be loved, into a present where that love still profoundly matters to us, but the behaviours associated with it are no longer possible. How someone achieves that is as unique as each life.

Largely through the work of Bowlby and Murray Parkes, the necessity of grieving is much better understood and respected than it was a generation ago. Each experience of bereavement is a per-sonal struggle, but it is also an instance of a response to loss, whose basic impulses are universal. Every society has created mourning customs to articulate the stages of grieving. Even in contemporary Western societies, where these customs have become so attenuated, we recognize that the bereaved need both support and permission to withdraw, to hold on to the meaning of the lost attachment and to take their time to re-engage with life. Family, friends, neighbours, colleagues at work, can all provide a network of relationships to help carry the bereaved through the everyday demands of life, when all their emotional energy is absorbed in coming to terms with loss. In so far as this network constitutes a community, or overlapping communities, with which the bereaved identifies, it can also formally or informally offer shared expressions of mourn-ing—not only in funerals, but memorials, anniversaries, celebra-tions of the dead. Such networks are not necessarily bounded by a particular place, but they are grounded in the familiar spaces of everyday life, and in bereavement, such places may become a symbol of continuity with the past. Loss of community, therefore, can be both a cause of grief, if it disrupts attachments, and make recovery from bereavement harder.

This understanding of grief has informed the hospice movement, through the conception of the hospice itself as a community where coming to terms with dying and loss is supported. But, for the most part, bereavement is seen as a misfortune of private life, beyond the reach of social intervention, except for the provision of bereavement counselling. Our politics rarely take account of grief as an issue for policy. We relegate it to the personal and private realms of experience. Yet, social and economic policies constantly affect communities, through redevelopment, changes in markets, investment, and production. Since the principles that inform these policies take no account of the uniqueness of the attachment bond, they often both promote loss and undermine support for recovery.

Social welfare in Britain, for instance, as it was designed after the Second World War, assumed that well-being, in so far as public policy could ensure it, depended on providing basic needs. Everyone should be guaranteed enough to eat, clothing and fuel to keep them warm, decent housing, education and health care, irrespective of his or her ability to pay for it. But in seeking to achieve these ideals, especially for housing, policies overlooked the ways in which they could disrupt attachments even more crucial to well-being. Slum clearance schemes tore families apart. Benefit rules conformed to the arcane logic of civil service accountability, indifferent to individual circumstance. Even in small ways, the desire to achieve an aggregate equity could hurt people, because it ignored the need for belonging and respect—aspects of well-being where attachments are crucial, as I discovered when I studied a sample of working class widows in London, most of them with children to bring up (Marris, 1958).

Their husbands' deaths threatened to undermine their identity as independent, married women. To lose that identity, becoming dependent upon family support, would have robbed them of a status that connected them to their dead husbands and to the life that they had shared. Yet, government policy at that time imposed a rule that severely limited how much a widow could earn without deductions from her pension. The policy responded to a Trade

Union concern that widows with pensions would drive down wages, since they might be willing to work for less. To address a notional risk, for which there was no evidence, the policy made it harder for the widows to sustain an identity that was crucial to the meaning of their lives, and to the working through of their grief.

Physiological needs for relief from hunger, cold, and sickness can be met in ways that are incompatible with psychological needs for identity, belonging, and meaning. The former can be satisfied by interchangeable and, therefore, quantifiable goods. One loaf of bread is equivalent to another; a gallon of heating oil is a measurable quantity of any such oil. One competent doctor can deliver most health care as well any other. But psychological needs are much more dependent on the presence and security of attachments. These are characteristically unique in their meaning, and thus irreplaceable. Progress in meeting physiological needs is much easier to measure: so many housing units built, wells dug, meals provided. It therefore receives far more attention than these other aspects of well-being, and even overrides them.

The administration of disaster relief illustrates this vividly, because a disastrous flood or hurricane may cause both widespread bereavement and an immediate crisis in food and shelter. How the needs arising from these very different kinds of trauma are reconciled and accommodated will have a profound, lasting effect on whether the victims can recover. Two instances of communities devastated by loss illustrate how the public response to a disaster can mitigate or aggravate bereavement. The way relief and reconstruction is administered can be as traumatic as the loss itself, if it ignores the attachments which constitute the meaning of people's lives.

Bereavement and disaster relief

In February 1972, a West Virginia mining valley called Buffalo Creek was overwhelmed when a dam burst, killing 125 men, women, and children and destroying the settlements along the valley floor. The disaster itself was horrifying: a wall of mud swept down the valley, carrying everything before it, flinging the bodies of its victims into trees and wreckage. But the aftermath led to a second bereavement more enduringly devastating than the dam burst itself, as Kai Erikson describes in his penetrating sociological analysis *Everything in Its Path* (Erikson, 1976). The Federal Department of Housing and Urban Development quickly took over the resettlement of the survivors, establishing them in mobile homes. Erikson writes,

> The net result of this procedure, however, was to take a community of people who were already scattered all over the hollow, already torn out of familiar neighborhoods, and make that condition permanent. . . . The camps served to stabilize one of the worst forms of disorganization resulting from the disaster by catching people in a moment of extreme dislocation and freezing them in a kind of holding pattern. [Erikson, 1976, p. 47).

This made psychological recovery very difficult, especially as the resilience of the community was already very fragile, following a long history of exploitation and dependency. Instead of supporting a process of working through grief to restore a sense of continuity and meaningful involvement in life, the resettlement frustrated it. The survivors seemed characteristically frightened, lonely, and grieving endlessly for a community they had no hope of recovering.

By contrast, another mining community, with a comparable history of exploitation and hardship, reacted to disaster much more positively. In October 1966, a tip from a disused coal mine above the Welsh village of Aberfan gave way, engulfing eighteen houses and a school, and killing 144 men, women, and children. The culture of the village—its Methodism, trade union socialism and vocational pride—was surely more robust than the Appalachian culture Erikson describes. But the most obvious difference is that the village itself was not destroyed and took charge, collectively, of its own recovery. It fiercely rejected the paternalistic attempts of government and outside professionals to manage either its grief or the millions of pounds subscribed for relief. It pressed the government and the National Coal Board to remove all the local tips, despite official assurances of their safety. From this arose a campaign to rehabilitate all the land that had been scarred by disused collieries and abandoned spoil heaps. Anger and guilt were discharged into a shared purpose, whose meaning derived from the cause of loss, giving Aberfan a renewed and even stronger sense of itself as a community (Miller, 1974).

No community, of course, however well integrated, can insulate its members from the trauma of bereavement. But an intact community represents a context of social continuity that can provide material support and routines of living to help carry the bereaved through times of emotional exhaustion and distress. It can help to articulate and validate the conflicting impulses of grief through its mourning customs. Above all, it represents a social world to which the bereaved still belongs, in which he or she is valued, and with which she is encouraged to re-engage as grief is worked through. Correspondingly, without such a community, recovery from bereavement is likely to be far more difficult and uncertain.

Community in this sense is not a place, or even necessarily narrowly bounded, but it is often vulnerable to disintegration if the places it inhabits are disrupted. When a disaster wipes out the site of a community, as in Buffalo Creek, or all along the shores of the Indian Ocean swept by the tsunami of December 2004, the vital need is to reconstitute the community so that it can provide the supportive framework for the working through of grief. This requires that the people who constitute this community are enabled to stay together, and this often means returning to the devastated site, which represents, even in dereliction, a continuity with the past—a place of remembrance—and perhaps still the ground of their livelihood. An account in the *New York Times* of 6 March 2005, describes how one Sri Lankan village sought to articulate their collective mourning:

> The present owes a debt to the past, the future to the present, so Hindus believe. Preserving the unbroken line of civilization means honoring that debt before moving forward; preserving peace for the living means satisfying the dead.
>
> And so, according to custom, 30 days after the tsunami the people of Navalady returned to their village, which had become a burial ground, to cook a feast for their relatives who had died. In family after family, the guests would be multiple.
>
> On the afternoon of the feast, a village which had been utterly bereft of life since the tsunami, began to stir with it. Families climbed off the boats that had brought them across the lagoon.

They dragged banana leaves as tall as men across the sand, and sat as if waiting for a picnic to begin. . . .

Around 6 p.m. the people of Navalady began to set out their meals. Pillyar Kannamuttu would have six lost loved ones at his feast, ranging from a 2-year-old granddaughter to his 34-year-old wife. The table was the foundation of a house he had given as a dowry for his youngest daughter, Uday Lakshmi. Both dowry and daughter were gone. . . .

Night came . . . Only small points of light—lanterns, candles, oil lamps, punctured the blackness. Each pointed to a mourning family, sitting in silence where its home had been.

This practice, carried on for centuries, was all the more important with an unnatural death, Mr Selvam, the body builder said. He did not want the wishes of his children's souls to go unfulfilled. They would come and eat to their hearts content. [Waldman, 2005]

This account is both moving and humbling—humbling because it suggests an extraordinary resilience in people who had lost so much, yet still had the strength to come together in this elaborate, age-old ritual of mourning. And that collective strength must surely be supportive and healing for each individual grief. But for something like this to happen, the community must be empowered to memorialize its loss and reconstitute its future in its own way. Eventually, some of its members will move away and find other communities. Navalady may never be rebuilt. But in the immediate aftermath of the disaster, amid such appalling loss, the community was still intact enough to provide an essential sense of continuity and meaning.

Unfortunately, the patterns and even the necessities of disaster relief are more likely to resemble what happened in Buffalo Creek than in Aberfan. The immediate needs are physical—food, water filtration plants, latrines, shelter, to bury the dead and prevent disease. All this has to be provided within a few days, and, in a major disaster, it becomes a large-scale logistical exercise. At the same time, millions, even hundreds of millions, of dollars in aid, prompted by sympathetic media accounts in countries around the world, have to be channelled and distributed. All this requires the organizational resources of governments, armies, and international relief organizations such as Oxfam, Doctors Without Borders, and the International Rescue Committee. The survivors of the disaster, disorientated and dispossessed, can play little or no part in this. They become dependent and often separated from each other by the hasty improvization of shelter. The longer they remain in this state, in what Erikson called a "holding pattern", the more demoralized they are likely to become. Temporary shelter becomes a refugee camp. And a refugee is defined by what he or she is escaping from, not what he is moving towards, because often there is nothing to foresee but the empty routines of a suspended life. Meanwhile, the children begin to adapt to the camp as their new place of belonging, but, without a productive economy, its opportunities may be mostly gambling, gang life, and crime.

So, it seems crucial that the surviving members of the community be provided with the resources, the authority, and the logistical support to take charge of their mourning and begin the process of reconstruction very quickly, before they become demoralized by endless delay. Since the recently bereaved, even in the best of circumstances, are vulnerable to feelings of apathy, withdrawal, and hopelessness, even a month of camp life, dependent on distant bureaucracies, with no apparent progress towards reconstruction, may undermine the will to work through grief. But all too often, once the immediate impulse of humanitarian relief is spent, politics, greed, and bureaucratic inertia reassert themselves. The villagers of Navalady have filled out endless forms—"They have come and written and written and gone," as one woman reported, "Everybody's writing endlessly" (Waldman, 2005, p. 22). But, meanwhile, the road to the village has not been rebuilt and none of the debris has been cleared. Neither the rebel Tamil Tigers further north nor the Buddhist government is politically invested in the region. In Aceh, in Indonesia, long in revolt against the central government, the situation is far worse. Disasters upset the balance of control, favouring the powerful. In Thailand, fishermen attempting to return to the site of their devastated village are met by armed guards, who tell them, "This is not your land. This land belongs to the Big Boss" (Mydans, 2005). The Big Boss is a developer who claims title to the land, overriding the villagers' customary rights, and plans to build a luxury tourist resort. Disasters often bring long-standing conflicts to a crisis of resolution, in which the victims of the disaster lack powerful advocates. Even sympathetic non-government relief organizations may be inhibited from intervening by their dependence on indifferent or hostile governments for access and logistical support.

The experience of disasters shows that sense of identity and belonging are extremely vulnerable to the loss of the places where they have been grounded. This is especially true of poorer people, who have fewer resources and less wide-ranging networks. But even when the community to which someone belongs is not local-ized, displacement can be disruptive, because our habits of connect-edness are always necessarily grounded. We move to a another part of the country, and find that we lose touch not only with friends in the place we left, but with other friends and interests elsewhere, who were once a part of our lives, but somehow do not reconnect to our new home. As the intricate network of relationships, which constitutes a way of life, is reconstituted in a new place, they come to be discarded. Communities of belonging, then, are not places, but they are more dependent upon places than is immediately apparent. And, in disasters, a place itself, even in its devastation, may be the only visible remnant of a community and thus a vital symbol of continuity with the past. Hence, to dispossess people permanently from the place they inhabited, for whatever reason, deprives them of crucial psychological and social resources to work through their grief.

Dispossession and economic change

What general conclusions can we draw from the experience of disasters? In many ways, the tsunami that engulfed the shores of the Indian Ocean was only a more sudden and immediately lethal equivalent of the wave of economic change that is sweeping over the whole world, disrupting and uprooting communities in the interests of productivity and profit. Fishermen are displaced by large-scale shrimp farms and tourist hotels, or the waters they fish in are poisoned by the mines of international conglomerates; logging companies erode the land. Indian farmers are committing suicide at unprecedented rates, unable to compete with global agri-business (Sengupta, 2006). Vast dams inundate thousand-year-old towns and villages. Slum clearance and gentrification force out the marginal contenders for a foothold in urban space. Or people are simply left behind as social and economic attrition drains the life out of the places they inhabit. Dispossession is a constant theme of growth. By the logic of economic development, this is progress, and, to be sure, the beautiful Thai beach, so conveniently swept of its traditional fishing community by the tsunami, will probably generate more wealth as a tourist resort, and some of the survivors may even find work there. But the calculations of economic development seldom take account of the psychological cost of this vast displacement. And these costs will come to haunt us as alienation, rage, humiliation, violence—all the ways that frustrated attachment seeks compensation and revenge.

When people are bereft of the communities to which they have belonged, the task of reconstituting a web of relationships to sustain a new life can be overwhelming. Their networks of mutual support have been disrupted, they may have lost most of their possessions, and they must struggle to find a foothold in a new, unfamiliar economy. And this puts great strain on attachments. It is hard to give a child love and attention when you are constantly anxious about the basic necessities of food, water, medicines, and shelter. The search for employment divides families and draws them away from home. Parents no longer represent reliable models of social competence and self-respect. The young people, alienated by their parents' demoralization and preoccupation with trying to make ends meet, will begin to look for a sense of meaning and self validation in peer groups that reject the humiliations and defeats their parents have endured. They may look for status in gangs, and for power through violence and the illegal economy, which offers them rewards the legitimate economy cannot match. This alienated generation is also attracted towards ideologies that offer an escape from the bewildering uncertainties and powerlessness of their circumstances. So, for instance, the orphaned Afghan refugees of decades of civil war grasp at the redemptive meaning of a puritanical Islam. Such ideologies are essentially other-worldly, in the sense that the community of faith they offer, with its rigid and uncompromising doctrine, is indifferent to the realities of everyday life. But that unworldliness also makes them impotent, except to justify acts of wholesale repudiation and destruction. Neither gangs nor ideological rigidity can sustain the kind of living, everyday, adaptive community able to support a family.

Communities in this sense are not places, but they are more grounded in specific places than we are often aware until we are dispossessed. The patterns of relationship that matter to us are also, characteristically, spatial patterns—journeys we habitually take, familiar encounters, proximities we take for granted in the day-to-day management of our lives. They come to have a cultural as well as a practical meaning, because of the relationships that inhabit them, and dispossession may give them an especial significance as sites of remembrance. This is why the displacement that so often accompanies economic development can be so traumatic.

In the now dominant ideology of economic growth, places are commodities—resources to be exploited for the highest return. They embody the possibilities of hydroelectric power, export crops, upscale housing; whatever use maximizes the potential profit. The present inhabitants stand in the way; the farmers and fishermen, slum dwellers, and householders scraping by. Such an idea of progress assumes that human adaptability has few limits. As economic assets are continually redistributed and reassembled, the wealth of society grows, so the argument runs, and everyone ultimately benefits, even if the process of adaptation to these changes may sometimes be painful.

People are certainly adaptable and resilient. But this resilience has conservative roots. It rests on an underlying confidence in attachment, and the strength of the understandings, purposes, and identities to which attachment has led. It is the adult counterpart of the way a child's readiness to explore depends on a secure base (Bowlby, 1988). People can withstand change and loss, perhaps even benefit from it, only if these essential assumptions remain intact. But uprooting typically undermines the whole structure of relationships, with all the meanings that have accrued to them, on which adaptation depends. Dispossession, therefore, may be a trauma from which its victims will never recover.

Our attachments are so central to our sense of who we are, to our purpose, to the communities to which we belong—to everything that constitutes the meaning of our lives—that the security of attachment is a crucial factor in every kind of relationship, from the interaction of mother and child to the dynamics of global capitalism.

An understanding of attachment needs, therefore, is as crucial to the practice of economic development as any economic theory. I have tried to show how the uniqueness of attachments explains what grieving has to accomplish, in answer to Freud's question, and how the communities to which the bereaved belong can support that task. Conversely, loss of community can both disrupt attachments and make recovery from bereavement harder. Because the guiding principles of economic progress do not acknowledge the uniqueness of attachments, or their fundamental importance for well-being, development often implies dispossession and lasting grief. That is not only a tragedy for its victims, but for the next generation, whose childhood will be crippled by the inability of the bereaved parents any longer to provide a secure attachment and sense of belonging. The frustration, anger, and alienation of that generation will, in turn, affect the way it confronts the world in adult life. So strategies of economic growth, which reallocate the resources of established communities or divert investment from them for the sake of immediately higher returns, risk such long-term damage to the cohesion and resilience of a society as to threaten its disintegration.

The way knowledge and the policy expertise it generates are organized in contemporary Western societies does not readily make these connections. Economists rarely talk to development psychologists; sociologists defend their intellectual territory from the encroachments of psychology. Intellectual inquiry tends to become more and more specialized, fragmenting into sub fields, each with its own jargon and shared assumptions. Correspondingly, policy guidance narrows to the controversies and applications of a particular intellectual discipline, whose sophistication pre-empts alternative approaches. But if we cannot find a way to make connections, such expertise will do great harm. So, in tracing what attachment theory implies for the way relationships act upon well-being, from the most intimate to the global, we not only rediscover these crucial connections, but make humane policies possible.

References

Bowlby, J. (1969). *Attachment and Loss, Volume 1: Attachment*. London: Hogarth.

Bowlby, J. (1973). *Attachment and Loss, Volume 3: Loss, Sadness and Depression*. London: Hogarth.

Bowlby, J. (1988). *A Secure Base: Clinical Applications of Attachment Theory*. London: Routledge.

Erikson, K. (1976). *Everything in its Path*. New York: Simon & Schuster.

Freud, S. (1917e). Mourning and melancholia. *S.E., 14*: 243–258. London: Hogarth.

Marris, P. (1958). *Widows and Their Families*. London: Routledge & Kegan Paul.

Miller, J. (1974). *Aberfan, A Disaster and its Aftermath*. London: Constable.

Mydans, S. (2005). Devastated by Tsunami, villagers fight builders for land. *New York Times*, 12 March.

Parkes, C. M. (1975). *Bereavement, Studies in Adult Grief*. Harmondsworth: Penguin.

Parkes, C. M., & Weiss, R. S. (1983). *Recovery from Bereavement*. New York: Basic Books.

Sengupta, S. (2006). On India's despairing farms, a plague of suicides. *New York Times*, 19 September.

Waldman, A. (2005). Torn from moorings, villagers grasp for past. *New York Times*, 6 March.

CHAPTER THREE

Labour to love

Marci Green

Human beings must labour to live. It is an essential life
activity on which the routine, and extraordinary, accom-
plishments of people and their societies depend. In the
first instance, labour makes life possible because we must produce
the goods and services we need to physically survive, like food,
clothing, and shelter. We also need to produce and distribute those
goods and services that enable our participation in the social and
cultural life of our families and communities.

For many of us, work shapes the rhythms of daily routine, and
we measure our movements by the sun, the seasons, the clock, the
tasks, and the contract. We labour in homes and backyards, factories, offices, on the land, in shops, in bars, in prisons, down mines,
in markets, on rubbish tips, in forests, in the sea, and on the streets.
The hours we work may be regular, or erratic, with better or worse
conditions of service and pay, autonomy, and control.

In most economies, work generates income, although much
work is unpaid. As well, it can be a source of social identity, security, social integration, and esteem. As a purposeful social activity,
work connects us with others in intimate or anonymous ways.
These relationships (with workmates, family, bosses, clients, and

customers) may give us, or diminish, our sense of worth. Furthermore, given the effort we might expend working over a lifetime, our experience of work can also shape our sense of ourselves and our conduct in public and private life

Work, therefore, is more than an activity. It is a social institution. Among other things, this means that it operates within broader "systems" of social networks, cultural ideas and beliefs, and economic relations. Thus, we do not work just as we please, or just to meet private needs. Furthermore, although it is ultimately our labour that sustains those systems, those systems, in turn, structure the conditions in which we work—and live—in significant ways. Thus, work may empower us, but it also has power over us.

Responsibility without control

Given the importance of work to society, and the effort people give over to it, it is useful to reflect on how little control many of us have over the organization and demands of the workplace, or the wider systems in which workplaces operate. By control, I mean the ability to "make things happen", to fashion our circumstances to adequately meet our needs. Within our places of work, we often have little say, for example, in the hours we work, whether or how much we are paid, whether we are hired or fired, and whether—and for how long—we have time to care for our children and other dependents, or get our own emotional needs met. This limited control is a source of tension, which we might manage by giving in to the demands of the job (and sacrificing too much of what matters outside the workplace) or leaving the job and putting ourselves and dependents at risk.

Some governments do legislate to provide basic protection of working conditions and entitlements (like a minimum wage, rights to collective representation, freedom from forced labour, health and safety provision, and maternity, paternity, and "compassionate" leave). However, even where workers' rights are formally established in the workplace (hard won through political struggle), in practice many employers may simply do as they wish. Furthermore, informal workplace cultures (the taken-for-granted norms, values, and assumptions about how we should perform our jobs) may undermine our courage to claim those rights to which we are entitled. For example, work cultures that are highly competitive and individualistic are often divisive, and distort our perception that work is a collective process. Such "non-relational" values (Fletcher, 1999; Hartling & Sparks, 2002) not only disrupt a shared sense of purpose within the workplace, but conceal the importance that other life interests and responsibilities (like sustaining friendships and families) hold for *all* of our workmates *and* for the larger communities in which we live. Bending our will to the culture of the workplace may bring us rewards, but sometimes at a cost to our emotional and social well-being.

In the context of the wider systems in which work is organized, our control is even more limited. For example, social inequalities relating to class, gender, colour, citizenship status, age, disability, and sexual preference are "systemic"; that is, they exist within and across our social institutions and cultures. Inequalities are generated by many social factors, not least of which are the popular perceptions and judgements about the differential value of human beings and their suitability to work. When these perceptions are mobilized in discriminatory ways, people's social and psychological resources are threatened as access to jobs, and the financial and honorarial rewards for doing them, are restricted.

There are other aspects of our wider systems that also diminish our control. For example, global movements of capital, product, and labour markets may weaken or destabilize local economies and communities. Changes to trade barriers, international exchange rates, conditions of State debt and financing, market pressures, and political conflicts will influence the economic environment in which enterprises are built, or broken (see Director-General's Report of the International Labour Conference of the ILO, 2006). Of course, changes can generate personal and community growth through the provision of new product markets and new jobs, the enhancement of workers' rights, a more stable local economy, improved social services, and a greater sense of self security. On the other hand, changes might disrupt our access to goods and services, leading to the decline of local resources and social networks and driving people out of their communities to seek work elsewhere (*ibid.*, pp. 18–29). In turn, this may lead to collective as well as individual insecurity, depression, and despair (Erikson, 1976; Marris, Chapter Two, this volume).

Thus, through work, we are locked into local, national, and global systems. Work links our private and public lives, our selves and society, in complex ways. But, the connections are rarely equitable, empowering, or just. However much the systems of work depend on our labour, and however much we depend on those systems to provide us with work opportunities, what is good for "the systems" may damage the people who keep them running. It is within this context, then, that we can begin to grasp some of the problems in making and maintaining the affectional bonds, and attachments in particular, that the institution of work helps create.

Bonds of attachment and affection

The claims that working makes on our physical, mental, and emotional resources have the potential to create real conflicts between the institutional demands of our work and our availability to others outside of work, especially if the public sphere of work is separated from our private lives (although, experientially, these two spheres are intimately connected). As well, our need *for* work generates conflicts of interest *within* individuals. Thus, the need for work might conflict with our more private need for our social and emotional health. It is important to consider these conflicts more closely, because they set the context for understanding why work is an attachment issue.

These conflicts appear in different forms, within and across societies. For example, what Sennett describes as new patterns of working in "late" capitalist societies illuminates the dis-ease these conflicts have generated (Sennett, 1999). He argues that they have not only weakened our ability to integrate work with other life activities, but have threatened to dissolve the conditions in which continuity of "self" and the capacity to build one's character can develop. While the patterns of working have long disrupted bonds of family and community through, say, enslavement and migration, what is "new" in recent years, Sennett argues, are the financial and honorarial rewards attached to "flexibility", episodic employment, job changes, work instability, and the disruptions to "life careers". These diminish the values of long-term commitment and loyalty, and change the nature of social bonds. In consequence, "the

qualities of good work are not the qualities of good character",
while friendship and local community acquire a "fugitive" status
(*ibid.*, p. 21).

Sennett's book exposes the sharp edges of the dilemma in which
so many people find themselves. That is, how do we work and also
make and maintain healthy connection? It is worth recalling, at this
point, some principles of attachment theory that will help us think
about this dilemma in a relational way.

According to attachment theory, central to emotional health and
development is the ability to meet our physical and emotional
needs. In the first years of life, infants' expressions of their attachment needs and their experiences of whether, and how well, their
needs are met will form the basis of their physical and emotional
health and an emerging sense of value and self-worth. These experiences will also begin to shape their own "internal" mental map for
navigating future affectional bonds.

One of the reasons why early attachment experiences are so
fundamental to human development is that they influence the
structure and processes of the brain (development is both nature
and nurture). Given that the earliest social environment is the relationship between the infant and primary care-giver(s), it is not
surprising that the quality of these early relationships is so important to an infant's growth

Over time, human beings become complex social selves through
more, or less, intimate social relationships. Attachments, however,
are special kinds of affectional bonds in which we invest our safety.
Especially in times of danger and distress, we will mobilize our
attachment behaviour to seek proximity to our attachment figures.
Both the availability (proximity) of the care-giver *and* the quality of
the care-giver's response to the infant's needs help to shape her
ability to regulate her internal physiological and emotional state,
her developing capacities to both trust and relate to others, and her
growing sense of security. (I use "her" merely for ease of expression.) Thus, humans—like other animals—establish a hierarchy of
attachment figures, even in communities where care-giving is
shared.

Secure attachments are those that are established by having our
attachment needs met in appropriate ways. By appropriate, we
mean those which regard the infant and child as a developing

person who needs loving regard, consistent care, soothing responses in times of distress, and emotional support as they struggle to balance their inner realities with the outside world (Winnicott, 1991). If our Attachment is secure, over time, a sense of self-security will come to reside *within* the developing child and adolescent as she participates in a variety of intimate, and, later, more public relationships.

If, however, those attachment needs are not met over time through, for example, unwanted separation from, or loss of, care-givers, inappropriate or inconsistent care-giving, physical and mental abuse and violations, a child's sense of self and relational abilities are likely be damaged.

Thus, a child's earliest experiences are particularly potent sources of personhood. Furthermore, given that attachment theory understands human beings developmentally, it argues that *attachments matter throughout life*. We can understand this idea in at least three ways. The first is that all human beings need the care, value, and regard of others, and we might seek proximity to a care-giver in times of danger, whatever our age. All human beings have "attachment needs" (even though the needs of infants will differ from those of healthy, securely attached adults).

The second way in which we understand that attachments matter throughout life has to do with the capacities we will have developed as adults to parent our own children, and to relate well enough to lovers, friends, and colleagues. These capacities will express those private, internal "working models" of relationships that we established early through our own attachment experiences. Adults who abuse others (and abuses can happen among work colleagues) are themselves likely to have experienced attachment failures early in life.

A third sense in which attachments matter throughout life reflects the understanding of our ability to develop a "secure base" within ourselves as we grow, even if our early attachment needs were not adequately met. Thus, experiences of being valued and loved by others in our wider family and social networks (including the workplace), can help to mediate, and afford some protection against, the effects of early attachment failures.

Given the importance of secure attachments for the kinds of people we will become, why is it that so many societies organize those essential life activities—such as work—in ways that inhibit our ability to make and maintain affectional bonds and secure attachments? Bowlby captures this concern in his claim that, while many societies recognize the importance of attachments, and value the work of parenting to meet appropriately the needs of children, "[p]aradoxically , it has taken the world's richest societies to ignore these basic facts" (Bowlby, 1993, p. 2). He elaborates by saying that

> Man and woman power devoted to the production of material goods counts a plus in all our economic indices. [However], [m]an and woman power devoted to the production of happy, healthy and self-reliant children in their own homes does not count at all. We have created a topsy-turvy world. [*ibid*.]

Work and relational security: three examples

Parents do not need to be schooled in attachment theory to understand the tensions between the demands of (and for) work and the affectional and attachment needs of their children, other dependents, and themselves. However, attachment theory helps us to tease out some of the various strands within those tensions, and to think about the possible consequences if those tensions are not resolved. How, then, might work influence our capacity to make and maintain our affectional bonds and sustain secure attachments? Let us consider three examples: the work–family "balance"; the problem of the transnational "love drain", and the experience of work as a "relational" environment.

Integrating work with family life

The theme of work–family balance goes to the heart of attachment dynamics. For this discussion, we will consider some examples of current working patterns in the UK. For most of us in employment, the common arrangement is that we work outside the home, usually for an agreed number of hours (although "flexible" working practices do operate), and in environments where conditions of work, pay, and family leave are set largely by the business. (Of course, many people, including children, work in their own family shops and businesses; these arrangements create their own variants of balancing work and affectional life.)

Parents' (and employers') anxieties have prompted social researchers to explore what they call the "work–family" balance. Since the late 1990s, for example, the Joseph Rowntree Foundation (JRF, UK) has funded numerous research projects to identify the tensions between conditions of work and family responsibilities, and the strategies that UK employers can adopt to alleviate the conflicts (Dex, 2003).

One of the developments over the past twenty-five years has been the increase in dual-earner households with dependent children (and older adults) (*ibid.*, pp. 10–12). This follows the general pattern over the past three decades of a steady rise in UK employment levels. Associated with the rise in dual-earner households, argue Crompton and Dennett, is the trend for mothers of young children to remain in paid employment. In 2001, for example, "57 per cent of mothers with children under five were in paid work" (Crompton and Dennett, 2003, p. 1).

In the Labour Market Review (2006), we find further data on current patterns. For example, in the spring of 2005, "working-age parents with dependent children . . . accounted for 35 per cent of the working-age population" (*ibid.*, p. 21). And, although historically, "couple mothers and lone parents . . . had lower employment rates than both couple fathers and working-age people without dependent children . . . the employment rate for couple mothers, couple fathers and lone parents has increased" (*ibid.*). Furthermore, employment rates among both couple mothers and lone parents with *pre-school age children* have also increased, representing a departure from past trends when those with pre-school children were less likely to be in full-time employment.

These data represent many developments, not least of which is the growing pressure on parents with dependents to work. Not surprisingly, part-time work has increased. This is not only because of the increase in the part-time labour market, and the decline in full-time options, but also because people are choosing to work fewer hours in the week (*ibid.*, p. 8; Walling, 2005). Furthermore, despite the trend in the reduction of working hours, there has been an increase in demand for non-parental care and paid care services (Dex, 2003, p. 12).

Parents know how hard it is juggle child-care (especially for pre-school children) and work obligations. This challenge arises pretty much from the time a child is born. There is great public and academic controversy over whether, and at what point, a return to work after the birth of a child is desirable, and what effects an early return might have on child and parents alike. None the less, for many of us, we often have little choice but to return to work as soon as possible. Back we go, even as our desire to be available for our children and our need to ensure the child's security may be painfully frustrated by the obligations that our jobs impose, especially since the quality of alternative child-care can be poor (*ibid.*, pp. 62–68).

In attachment terms, these working patterns raise issues for a child's proximity to a care-giver, and for consistency and for quality of care that can be provided. (There is also the matter, of course, of the parents' need to be with their children.) For example, a parent's availability to a child will obviously be limited by work commitments, although the age and experiences of the child may mediate a child's experience of, and ability to manage, a parent's absence. However, for infants, in particular, attachment theory argues that *not any carer* will do, particularly when the child is in distress. After all, children in distress are seeking proximity to their attachment figures and have established their hierarchy of those in whom they invest their safety. Parents may make alternative care arrangements—with family, friends, child-minder or nursery—but the consistency and quality of this care certainly matters.

Given the data on the increase in the number of working parents with very young children, there are some grounds for concern about the risks to the child's development in her early years and the effects that alternative care arrangements may have on the attachment bonds between infant and working parents, Working parents struggle to accommodate a child's needs—many successfully—as the growth in "flexible" and "atypical" (by "atypical", I mean outside the hours of 9 a.m. to 6 p.m.) arrangements demonstrates (see, for example, La Valle and colleagues, cited in Dex, 2003, p. 13; Houston & Waumsley, 2003; Statham & Mooney, 2003). Unfortunately, good quality alternative care is problematic (Dex, 2003, pp. 74–75).

Of course, there is no guarantee that a parent to whom a child has ready access will necessarily be able to meet adequately the child's attachment needs. As we know, the capacity to parent "well enough" has as much to do with parents' own early attachment experiences as with the institutional and cultural environment in which they live as adults. In terms of work experiences, however, a parent exhausted as a result of long or erratic hours on low (or even good) pay, in a competitive and individualist work culture, struggling to meet "targets", enduring monotonous tasks, and working for an employer whose style of management is modelled on Rambo, might be physically available to build a child's experience of security but be emotionally unable to do so. Consistent and appropriate care-giving requires health, patience, strength, and imaginative energy, not least because the needs of an infant and growing child change rapidly and require sensitive and appropriate responses.

Given the dilemma of needing work and rearing children, who, then, takes care of care-giving? A primary care-giver, if possible. If not, then the main care-giver's family, friends, neighbours, childminders, and nursery staff. However, as the JRF research suggests, the need for child-care in the UK has outstripped the supply, especially in families without support networks or the financial resources to buy good quality care. In other words, there is a "care deficit" in Britain. This deficit, however, has no national or class boundaries, and its conditions and effects are global.

The transnational "love drain"

In *Global Women* (Ehrenreich & Hochschild, 2003), Parrenas argues that

> [a] growing crisis of care troubles the world's most developed nations. Even as demand for care has increased, its supply has dwindled. The result is a care deficit to which women . . . (largely from developing countries) . . . have responded in force. [Parrenas, 2003, p. 39]

Helping to meet the deficit are mostly women who tend to be poorly paid, with few working rights and protections (Hondagneu-Sotelo, 2003, pp. 55–69), who may be politically vulnerable, and, often, are mothers of children left behind in their country of origin. These women comprise the flow of an international "love drain", and as the flow increases to meet one deficit, it helps to create another.

Given that proximity, consistency and quality of care are germane to a child's development, what do we make of global systems that drive third world women to seek work raising 'first world' children. Parrenas (2003) describes, for example, the migration of Filipino women to developed nations; when these women are mothers, "they leave behind their own children, usually in the care of other women" (*ibid.*, p. 39). Acknowledging the vital contribution that remittances from migrant workers make to the Philippine's economy and the survival of impoverished Filipino communities, the author then considers what this love drain can mean for Filipino mothers and their children (*ibid.*, pp. 39–40).

One Filipina interviewed by Parrenas migrated to Rome to work as a nanny, "caring for other people's children while being unable to tend to [her] own" (*ibid.*, p. 41). This mother said,

> When the girl that I take care of [in Rome] calls her mother "Mama", my heart jumps all the time because my children also call me "mama". I feel the gap caused by our physical separation especially in the morning when I pack [her] lunch, because that's what I used to do for my children ... I used to do that very same thing for them. I begin thinking that at this hour I should be taking care of my very own children and not someone else's, someone who is not related to me in any way, shape or form ... The work that I do here is done for my family, but the problem is they are not close to me but are far away in the Philippines. Sometimes, you feel the separation and you start to cry ... Sometimes, when I receive a letter from my children telling me that they are sick, I look up out the window and ask the Lord to look after them and make sure they get better even without me around to care after them ... If I had wings, I would fly home to my children. Just for a moment, to see my children and take care of their needs, help them, then fly back over here to continue my work. [*ibid.*, pp. 41–42]

The child of another Filipina, who was working as a domestic in New York City, talked of the pain of separation.

> There are times when you want to talk to her [mother] but she is not there. That is really hard, very difficult ... There are times when I want to call her, speak to her, cry to her, and I cannot. It is difficult.

> The only thing that I can do is write to her. And I cannot cry through the e-mails and sometimes I just want to cry on her shoulder. [*ibid.*, p. 42]

There are so many children whose mothers are at great distances caring for others (Ehrenreich & Hochschild, 2003, pp. 1–13), and it takes enormous effort to manage their deep yearning for their mother's (and father's) presence. Parrenas describes the ways that children often repress their feelings because they know that mother's income makes life in the Philippines possible. That many of the children and parents "manage" the separation emotionally (and the author suggests that parents can "be there", even at great distances), is testimony to, among other things, the importance of affectional bonds in the community, surrogate parenting, and the child's recognition of the importance of the distant mother's work. However, many other children simply lack these resources.

We can glimpse the magnitude of the potential care deficit to which Parrenas refers from a recent Conference Report of the International Labour Organisation (Director-General, 2006). The Director-General reports that

> [m]igrant workers, of whom women now represent nearly half, constitute a growing share of the world's workforce. In 2000 there were more than 86 million migrant workers throughout the world, with 34 million of these in developing regions. . . . From 1985 to 1995, the number of international migrants increased by nearly 6 million a year, a faster rate of growth than that of the world's population. [*ibid.*, p. 26]

Furthermore, while the report recognizes that there are real benefits to women's migration,

> [a]t the same time, women tend to be restricted to jobs associated with their traditional "female roles" such as caregivers, nurses and domestics. Similarly, migrant women are more vulnerable to particular forms of gender-specific violence and sexual abuse, especially when working as domestics and sex workers. [Chen et al. (2005), cited in Conference Report of the International Labour Organisation, 2006, p. 27]

From an attachment perspective, there are many questions we need to ask about the immediate and long-term effects on brain development, and the emotional health of persons, families, and communities that this love drain generates. For instance, how well does a child comfortably distinguish between an absent parent and one who has abandoned them? How well can surrogates meet a young child's need for proximity, consistency, and quality of care? How truly resilient are children to long separations from parents? And how well will those children be able to parent themselves and their own future children? In what ways do the cultures of the parents' communities provide ways of making sense of prolonged absences? Are the costs acknowledged or concealed by families, communities, and governments? Furthermore, what of the emotional state of the transnational mother, especially given that, in many countries, the care drain falls so heavily on the shoulders of women (whose social and political status is "second class", on whom the responsibility for the care of their own and others' children still largely rests, and who may be suffering violence and sexual abuse). One also wonders, not least, about the security of attachments between the "first world" infant, her transnational care-giver, and that infant's own parents.

The workplace as a relational environment

The themes of work–family balance and the love drain have allowed us to glimpse some of the problems that work can create for enabling secure attachments. That is, the focus up to now has been on integrating work demands with family relationships. But, clearly, not all workers are parents, or have other family commitments. Furthermore, given the importance of the workplace itself as a "relational environment" in which we might, as adults, come to invest our security (and to which we might retreat from family life!), it is important to consider those work-based processes and arrangements that could influence an adult's sense of self security and esteem.

For example, there are growing pressures in many societies for employees to work overtime, be "on call", be geographically mobile, and to work short-term, episodic, project-based contracts. The rewards for accommodating this powerful and seductive culture of work are often high, but at what emotional cost? For one thing, one's career may be marked by periods of intense labour alternating with bouts of unemployment, making it hard to plan for the future. Although not without benefits, such arrangements may lead over time to emotional and social insecurity. For another, the new work culture can inhibit the opportunities to establish and sustain meaningful social networks and affectional bonds, especially if our contracts require long periods away from friends and family. This is more a problem of "work/life" than work–family balance, where the rewards accrue from living to work, rather than working to make the rest of life possible. Then, too, competitive work cultures may discourage us from claiming, say, maternity, paternity, and compassionate leave. It is sobering to think that the intensification of work pressures and the sacrifices these entail can heighten our need for affectional bonds while depriving us of the very opportunities we need to sustain them.

Workplaces may also diminish one's sense of self-value and esteem. For example, studies by colleagues at Wellesley College in the USA argue that corporate work environments in America tend to be extremely competitive, individualistic, and rationalistic (whereby only that which can be "measured" matters to the organization). These public "non-relational" norms of the workplace prevail, despite the fact that work is a collective, co-operative activity.

For example, Fletcher (1999) explores the cultures of work as they relate to gender. In her research on a hi-tech company in the USA, she demonstrates that gender matters significantly in the recognition we get for our work, and that much of the labour that women contribute is "disappeared" by the firm. Women are more likely than men to work relationally and to acknowledge the co-operative nature of their efforts, but the rewards tend to accrue to those who claim sole authorship of their achievements. Thus, to "succeed" at work as individuals might require us to conceal the contributions of others and to publicly separate ourselves from those on whom our ability to do our jobs really depends. In other words, in order to contribute to the work of the firm, one might become disconnected from others, and to be seen to have achieved competitively, one might become disconnected from oneself.

Other research argues that women often provide "emotional labour", for which is there is little recognition or reward. Emotional labour entails the routine management of one's own feelings and the emotional needs of clients, colleagues (and bosses). For example, Hochschild (1983, 2003) argues that emotional labour is embedded in workplace culture and practices, yet it is often taken for granted and unacknowledged. One reason why emotional labour is undervalued is because it is hard to measure; it does not yield to the format of a spreadsheet. Another reason why emotional labour—expended usually by women—is undervalued is because it is something that women are perceived to "do naturally". In societies where the perception of skill is restricted to particular kinds of *acquired* knowledge (assumed to be held by men), "natural endowments" are seen to need no effort. (This, despite the fact that the relational knowledge that emotional labour requires is accumulated over many years.) Since the culture of many firms links effort with reward (in theory if not in practice), it is no surprise that women's emotional labour is largely invisible.

For females struggling for selfhood in society, such conditions in the workplace can reproduce the sense of impotence and inferiority that sexism in our culture generates. On the other hand, work will provide income and might deliver some social esteem and security. Work, therefore, can both enhance and diminish our sense of worth. In so far as work can be a source of relational valuing (and we can attach to organizations as we do to people), we may seek our security in the very place that can also undermine it. This is the case, of course, for all of us who work in conditions of social inequality.

Summary and conclusion

Work is an essential life activity, and so, too, is the process of enabling and maintaining attachments and affectional bonds. Both are important sources of security and identity, but they can make powerfully conflicting claims on our material, physical, and emotional resources. Unfortunately, in many societies, work takes priority financially and culturally over our efforts to grow (and to be) securely attached human beings, and our institutions do little to enable the conditions necessary to lessen the emotional wreckage that comes from failed attachments.

Many of us will struggle to resolve the tensions that both work and care-giving may generate, and as individuals we will achieve this with varying degrees of success. But the responsibilities for the health of persons and communities cannot rest on the shoulders of individual care-givers because our work activities, and our capacities to give and receive appropriate care, are influenced by the institutional arrangements, cultural systems, and the economies over which we have little control.

We may also struggle to find value in a workplace where the culture and systems of rewards may discourage co-operation and mutual regard. Such non-relational environments may undermine emotional security even as they provide the financial resources on which we depend. Certainly, work can provide us with ways of making life meaningful, and may provide a secure base from which we operate. However, relational values and practices are rarely the organizing principles of work environments.

It is important to recognize that there *are* policy makers and employers in some countries who are seeking ways of balancing work and care-giving needs, with much of the pressure for these initiatives coming from parents (in the UK, see, for example, Dex, 2003; Yeandle, Crompton, Wigfield, & Dennett, 2002). That pressure must continue. But, one of the problems we face in enabling change is establishing where that balance should be struck, especially in societies that take as the norm the principles of production and profit (Miller, 1984).

Of course, the connections between patterns of work and our ability to give and get care varies within and across societies. In some countries, the organization of work is brutal, especially in states whose authorities condone the practices of child labour, forced labour, and the trafficking of migrant workers (see UNICEF, 2005). These conditions can certainly induce levels of both collective and individual trauma that most workers in the UK, for example, might not experience, but even here in Britain there is no room for complacency.

Evidence of growing social pathologies in many societies should alert us to the real risks to emotional and social health that arise from insufficient regard for the role that attachment experiences play in the kinds of people we become and our capacities to parent our own children. The responsibility for safeguarding the conditions that enable affectional bonds and secure attachments must be collectively held. Change towards this end is possible, and there are national and international bodies working to create it. I believe that a shared public understanding of the importance of secure attachments for human development is needed to enhance that process.

References

Bowlby, J. (1993). *A Secure Base: Clinical Applications of Attachment Theory*. London: Routledge.

Chen, M., Vanek, J., Lund, F., Heintz, J., Jhabvala, R., & Bonner, C. (2005). *Progress of the World's Women: Women, Work and Poverty*. New York: UNIFEM.

Crompton, R., & Dennett, J. (2003). Organisations, careers and caring. *Joseph Rowntree Foundation Report*, www.jrf.org.uk/knowledge/findings/socialpoliy/n33.asp

Dex, S. (2003). *Families and Work in the Twenty-First Century*. London: Joseph Rowntree Foundation.

Director-General's Report (2006). Changing patterns in the world of work. International Labour Conference. Geneva.

Ehrenreich, B., & Hochschild, A. R. (Eds.) (2003). *Global Women*. London: Granta.

Erikson, K. (1976). *Everything in its Path*. New York: Simon and Schuster.

Fletcher, J. (1999). *Disappearing Acts: Gender, Power, and Relational Practice at Work*. Cambridge, MA: MIT.

Hartling, L., & Sparks, E. (2002). Relational–cultural practice: working in a nonrelational world. *Stone Center Work in Progress*, No. 97. Wellesley, MA: Wellesley Centers for Women.

Hochschild, A. R. (1983). *The Managed Heart: Commercialization of Human Feeling*. Berkeley, CA: University of California Press.

Hochschild, A. R. (2003). *The Commercialization of Intimate Life: Notes from Home and Work*. Berkeley, CA: University of California Press.

Hondagnu-Sotelo, P. (2003). Blowups and other unhappy endings. In: B. Ehrenreich & A. R. Hochschild (Eds.), *Global Women* (pp. 00–00). London: Granta.

Houston, D., & Waumsley, J. (2003). Attitudes to flexible working and family life. *Joseph Rowntree Foundation Report*. New York: Meridien/New American Library.

Labour Market Review (2006). Office for National Statistics. London: Palgrave/Macmillan.

Miller, A. (1984). *Thou Shalt Not Be Aware*. New York: Farrar, Straus and Giroux.

Parrenas, R. S. (2003). The care crisis in the Philippines: children and transnational families in the new global economy. In: B. Ehrenreich & A. Russell Hochschild (Eds.), *Global Women* (pp. 39–54). London: Granta.

Sennett, R. (1999). *The Corrosion of Character: The Personal Consequences of Work in the New Capitalism.* New York: W. W. Norton.

Statham, J., & Mooney, A. (2003). *Around the Clock: Childcare Services at Atypical Times.* London: Joseph Rowntree Foundation/Policy Press. Also available at: www.jrf.org.uk/knowledge/findings/socialpolicy (accessed June 2003).

UNICEF (2005). Child labour today. Available at: www.unicef.org/brazil/estudo_uk.pdf

Walling, A. (2005). Families and work, *Labour Market Trends, 113*(7): 275–283. National statistics online, www.statistics.gov.uk/cci/article.asp?ID=1192&POS=3&olRank=1& Rank=1.

Winnicott, D. W. (1991). *The Child, the Family and the Outside World.* London: Penguin.

Yeandle, S., Crompton, R., Wigfield, A., & Dennett, J. (2002). Employers, communities and family-friendly employment policies. *Joseph Rowntree Foundation Report*, www.jrf.org.uk/knowledge/findings/socialpolicy.

CHAPTER FOUR

Unsettling policies: unanticipated consequences for migrant Afro-Caribbean families

Elaine Arnold

Introduction

> Perhaps in their day work, whether with disturbed children, disturbed adults, or disturbed families, clinicians have of necessity to view causal processes backwards, from the disturbance of today back to the events and conditions of yesterday. [Bowlby, 1973, p. xi]

When people from the Caribbean were recruited to work in Britain after the Second World War, they could not have anticipated the devastating effects that their experiences of broken attachments, separation, and loss of all that was familiar would have upon them. Neither were they prepared for the failure by the British Government to help them meet their basic needs for housing and welfare, nor for the often hostile reception they received from the local population. This chapter will consider some of the experiences of Afro-Caribbean workers and their families of migration to, and settlement in, the UK.

In the aftermath of the Second World War, John Bowlby was ideally placed to study the effects on children of separation from their mothers when he was commissioned by the World Health

Organisation to conduct a study of the mental health aspects of the needs of homeless children. These were described as "children who were orphaned or separated from their families for other reasons and needed care in foster homes, institutions or other types of group care" (Bowlby, 1952, p. 45) He visited several European countries and the USA, where he consulted with workers involved in child care and child guidance work, and studied the available literature. On the basis of the evidence discovered, Bowlby concluded that the break-up of family played a decisive role in the character development of children.

Some of the work that informed Bowlby's research was the first recorded observations of young children who were separated from their mothers and cared for in the Hampstead nurseries in London. Anna Freud observed that, upon separation, the children at first seemed dazed, and then indifferent to their surroundings for several days. Their behaviour then became turbulent. Their physical health was undermined and they suffered from colds and intestinal problems. Very many refused to be handled or comforted by strangers and "for several hours, or even a day or two, this psychological craving of the child, the 'hunger for his mother' [seem to override] all bodily sensations" (Freud & Burlingham, 1974, pp. 182–183).

James Robertson, a social worker who had worked at the Hampstead nurseries, joined Bowlby's research team and spent a great deal of time observing children who, upon admittance to hospital, were separated from their parents. Robertson noted three phases of the children's reactions. The first of these was *protest*, when the children cried and attempted to maintain proximity to mother by looking at and trying to access the door through which mother had left. This was followed by *despair*, when the children realized that mother had not responded by returning; they whimpered, became listless, and showed no interest in playing or responding to the nurses—as if they had entered a state of mourning. As time passed, the children then became *detached*; they no longer rejected the adults who were available, but related superficially and seemed indifferent to their presence. When mothers came to visit, their children appeared uninterested, adopted a superficial cheerfulness, and focused on the presents that the mothers would bring.

Bowlby and Robertson sought to raise awareness with members of the caring profession about the traumatic reactions of children to the experience of separation. However, they encountered considerable resistance. Undaunted, they collaborated and produced a film, *A Two-Year-Old Goes to Hospital* (Robertson, 1969), which demonstrated their observations. Robertson then toured the USA and presented his work. As a result, many of the hospitals there changed their policies on parental visits. Spurred on by this success, Bowlby and Robertson continued their campaign for a change of policy to allow mothers to stay in hospital with their sick children.

Bowlby was also influenced by Marris's study of the responses by widows to the deaths of their husbands (1958). Their reactions included anger (sometimes directed towards others or the absent person), a searching for the person lost, and disbelief. Professionals often labelled such reactions as "denial", a description with which both Marris and Bowlby disagreed. Bowlby combined Marris's insights with his own additional observations of children's reactions to unwanted separation and loss (through hospitalization, evacuation, and institutional placement). He concluded that the responses of children to separation from primary care-givers were similar to those of adults in mourning, as well as to those adults who had not resolved the trauma of separation from which they had suffered in their early lives (Bowlby, 1969).

Bowlby's position was severely criticized at the time, but came to be vindicated through the work of others (e.g., Parkes, 1978). It was a position that came to express one of the fundamental principles of attachment theory. That is, that the experiences of unwanted separation and loss of attachments and affectional bonds exert a profound influence on the emotional health of persons throughout the life span.

I shall explore this principle in relation to the lives of Afro-Caribbean people who migrated to Britain after the Second World War.

The migration experience: historical background

In considering the experiences and consequences of separation and loss within families of African-Caribbean origin, it is important to set this discussion in some historical context. This context is not just about the movement of persons from one country to another and the trauma that such movement often created. It also helps us to understand the reasons why people were willing to disrupt their relationships of kin and community. Then, too, it exposes the effects upon individuals and families of the experiences of racist hostility from every level of the communities in which they settled—experiences that deepened the sense of isolation and loss.

When immigration from the Caribbean to Britain began to increase in the 1950s, the growth in the number of black people (i.e., with one or both parents conventionally regarded as black) tended to give the impression that their presence was an entirely recent phenomenon. This was not so, for small numbers of black people were retained as servants in some households of affluent white citizens during the sixteenth, seventeenth, and eighteenth centuries, when having black servants was considered to be fashionable (as evidenced in some of the paintings by Joshua Reynolds). These black people had been slaves; some of them had been taken directly from Africa, while others were brought by slave owners from the Caribbean islands.

The black population increased when those who had fought for the British in the American War of Independence, 1775–1783, and in the Anglo-French wars in the West Indies, 1786–1787, came to Britain and settled in various parts of the country, mainly in seaport towns and cities. Many lived in London, and it is alleged that in 1764 there were approximately 20,000 black people out of a population of 676,000 living there (*The Gentleman's Magazine*, 1764).

When black servants in Britain chose to leave the service of the aristocracy and live independently, it was difficult for them to obtain work, despite the fact that many possessed skills in various trades. Subsequently, they were reduced to living in poverty, dependent on the Poor Law benefits. This fuelled an exaggerated perception in Britain that black people were mainly from the lower socio-economic level of society, poor and unskilled, eking out an existence on the dole. Unfortunately, the stereotype lingered in the minds of many of the indigenous population, and helped to shape the policies and practices of public institutions as well as the quality of interpersonal relations.

After the First World War, 1914–1918, the black population in the UK increased through the presence of students from the colonies who came over to study for the recognized professions. However, their contacts were limited mainly to the teaching staff in universities and other teaching institutions, and with landlords and landladies, leaving little opportunity for real engagement with the wider British population. It was not generally known that some of the students from the Caribbean were scholarship winners funded by their governments, who, upon graduation, were bound by contract to return to their various countries to practise their professions. Others were people of dual heritage, the offspring of unions between fathers who were white plantation owners and black women. Some fathers accepted the responsibility for educating their children and sent them to schools and universities in the UK.

When these English-educated professionals completed their qualifications, they returned to their islands. There, they formed the middle classes of the society and were regarded by the population as role models for their children. Education was considered as the means for social, economic, and political advancement. In time, when independence from Britain's colonial rule was achieved in some of the countries, there were men and women who were not only well educated, but who possessed confidence in their ability to replace the white English colonists in positions of power and authority within their home governments.

During the Second World War, 1939–1945, Britain appealed to her colonies for help with the plaintive cry, "The Mother Country needs you". This appeal spoke to the hearts of men and women from the Caribbean reared in a culture which honoured the mother. (I raise the issue, here, of the power of the "mother" bond as represented in the idea of the "mother country". From the perspective of attachment theory, I think that power is considerable, yet the emotional dimension of the concept "mother country" is rarely understood or acknowledged in the literature.) People were also motivated to respond to Britain's plea by their deep spirit of adventure, love of travel outside the Caribbean territories, and the severe economic problems of their islands, where poverty was rife and employment prospects limited.

Seven thousand men joined the Royal Air Force, and were reasonably treated by the Colonial Office as Britain was grateful for their presence (Bonham-Carter, 1987). Others were recruited to work as technicians in the various factories in the war industry and in forestry, but they were made redundant upon the return of indigenous ex-servicemen and the developing economic crisis of 1947.

Women had also declared their interests to serve in the war, and applied to join the armed forces. However, according to Bousquet and Douglas (1991, pp. 82–126), the War Office initially objected to the recruitment of black women. This objection—a strong mix of racist and sexist attitudes—generated lengthy and acrimonious debates within the Colonial Office. For example, on the one hand the Colonial Office was reluctant to prevent black women from joining the armed forces in case it revived strong political opposition in the colonies, where uprisings had occurred prior to the outbreak of war. On the other hand, the Colonial Office was bowing to pressure from the US government once America entered the war; the USA had long operated a "colour bar", and, during the war, it discriminated against black women who volunteered to serve in Washington (only white women from the Caribbean were recruited for the Auxiliary Women's Service).

However, as the war dragged on and help was needed desperately in all of the Services, black women were enlisted in the Auxiliary Territorial Services and served in the UK. The women recruited from the Caribbean countries were from the middle classes and from among those who had become socially mobile through education. However, despite their qualifications and skills, the armed services did not guarantee proper deployment. "At every stage of recruitment and deployment, race was a pre-eminent issue" (Bousquet & Douglas, 1991, p. 126).

Clearly, anti-black racism featured strongly in the thinking of government officials. Even in the war against fascism they were reluctant to employ black people who had demonstrated their political loyalties. While some of the British population were friendly with black servicewomen during the war, a return to civilian life exposed black women to a revival of racism and discrimination (*ibid.*, p 142). This pattern was repeated in the years after the war, when black immigrants were first welcomed as useful labour but were then subjected to racist hostility.

Britain was severely damaged during the war, and the government sought to re-establish itself as a world economic power. Changes in the post-war industrial structure of the country and the labour market meant there were labour shortages in manufacturing and service jobs. Just as the government during the war recruited overseas colonial subjects for the war effort, employers—with government assistance—appealed for overseas workers to work in industries such as health, transport, catering, the foundries, and garment production. Since there was widespread unemployment in the colonies, and Britain was unable at that time to divert resources towards the colonies' economic development, overseas British subjects responded to the government's initiatives

Another factor that influenced the immigration from the Caribbean was the passing of the McCarran Act (1952) in the USA, which limited the number of migrants entering that country. This was a severe blow to Afro-Caribbean workers, as the USA had been a popular place for those seeking employment in the service industries. So it was that when Britain turned to the West Indies to recruit labour, the people were eager to respond to the call. The invitation also activated their affection for the "Mother Country", as it had when they volunteered with alacrity to fight during the two world wars.

Under the British Nationality Act of 1948, immigrants from all the British colonies held British passports issued by the governments of those colonies, and, in the immediate post-war period, they were free to enter the UK as British citizens. However, within two decades after mass immigration had begun, the UK government had substantially cut immigration of Afro-Caribbean and Asian immigrants. This began with the passing of the Commonwealth Immigration Act, 1962. In so doing, the government fed a growing culture of anti-black racism, through which the term "immigrant" became synonymous with "black", and "blackness" was linked with poverty and crime. There emerged, too, a growing "moral panic" about a "black presence", which was conceived as a threat to British national identity. Such public and political perceptions of colonial subjects from African/Caribbean (and Asian) origins textured the institutions and culture of British society and threatened to deepen the sense of separation and loss from which so many migrant workers already suffered.

Settling in and surviving

In my research and clinical practice at Nafsiyat (Mind, Body and Soul) Intercultural Therapy Centre in London, over the years I have had many conversations with numerous people who arrived during the early days of post-war immigration. Most of them had envisaged a temporary stay in Britain (for example, Arnold, 2001; Robertson, 1975). Information they received during the recruitment drive for labour had led them to believe that, with full employment, it would be possible to accumulate sufficient financial resources to return home and better their economic situations. It seems that their primary motive was to meet their material needs. That, combined with the belief that their stay in the UK would be for a limited time, helped them to repress the emotional dimensions and consequences of their separation from, and loss of, family, home, and friends.

Unfortunately, many of the people who had planned to return home after a relatively short stay in Britain were unable to do so. Many of the immigrants were employed as manual workers, and on wages lower than those earned by the indigenous population. This meant great financial struggle in Britain, leaving few resources with which to return home comfortably. Moreover, as Afro-Caribbean families had fled the poverty of the Caribbean for a better life, they were loath to return to the very conditions they had left. Many never abandoned their dream of life back in Caribbean, but the dream became hard to sustain. Problems of employment and income undermined people's plans, and fuelled a sense of loss. So, too, did other experiences that settling in Britain entailed.

Financial insecurity can undermine emotional well-being. It puts at risk the capacity to feed, clothe, and shelter oneself and one's family, and to participate in the social life of a community—in this case, a community made tenuous by racist hostility. But these were not the only conditions that undermined emotional stability. Problems with housing and child-care added more burdens to the effort to survive, and threatened the quality of attachments within families.

Housing

There are many examples of the role played by inadequate housing provision on the living standards and emotional health of populations. For instance, in South London, where many immigrants had settled, the government had not considered it feasible to provide housing for newcomers, especially when local people were also in need. Furthermore, many white house owners were reluctant to accept black people as tenants (Peach, 1968, p. 87). Poor and substandard housing existed in South London, as in other inner cities, and since the new migrants were so poorly paid, they had no alternative but to accept what was available. According to the 1967 PEP Report on Racial Discrimination, when the borough councils in the city housed the immigrants they were usually allocated the poorest houses in old council (municipal) estates and in areas where they were subjected to persistent racial abuse and physical attacks (as cited in Peach, 1968, p. 85).

In a study conducted in 1965 of one-year-old children of "West Indian Immigrants" living in Paddington, London, Hood and colleagues described conditions in the following way.

> A typical example of the kind of housing in which the study families were living is that of a drab two or three storey house built in the late 1800s that has been divided into ten to twenty single, lofty, sparsely furnished, dully decorated and unheated rooms. A double-ring gas burner might be able on the landing to be shared by most of the people on that floor, as might be a solitary bathroom and lavatory. [Hood, Oppe, Pless, & Apte, 1970, p. 5]

The authors of the study expressed the view that the families did their best in creating clean and tidy homes in their one room, and strongly opposed the racist public perceptions that Black migrant families were responsible for, and happy to live with, the squalid surroundings in which they found themselves (*ibid.*, p. 40).

Another study looked at the problems of accommodation in flats (apartments). According to Osborn and Butler (1985), who undertook comparative research of children born in 1970 to European, Afro-Caribbean or Indian/Pakistan families, flats were the least desirable accommodation for families with young children. For one thing, mothers with prams and pushchairs, or heavy shopping, found it difficult to negotiate stairways when lifts were broken (as they often were). Also, some of the council flats were so poorly designed that when it rained the balconies were flooded and it was difficult to leave or enter without becoming wet. Such problems clearly curtailed the opportunities for parents to take their children outdoors, to shop, and to meet with other mothers and children on the council estates. This situation placed more stress on mothers and undermined the emotional resources they had to meet their children's needs.

My own research with mothers (Robertson, 1975) anticipated the concerns raised by Osborn and Butler. One interviewee, "Mrs B" (now comfortably housed in the family's own home), recalled the early days, after they arrived from the Caribbean. She told me that

> We were cooped up in one room in a flat. This was so unpleasant; the bed here, the stove there, cooking, washing doing everything in the same place. I just could not understand how we could live like that. We moved several times, never comfortable, never happy.

Importantly, too, Osborn and Butler found that Afro-Caribbean families were more likely to be housed in flats than were those of other nationalities; forty per cent of the children of Afro-Caribbean children lived in flats, maisonettes, or self-contained rooms, compared with 10.2% of European and 10.8% of Indian/Pakistani children (Osborn & Butler, 1985, p. 35).

Osborn and Butler warned of the problems that such poor environments could generate for the health and normal development of growing children. They expressed the view that "their detrimental effects may contribute significantly to the educational or behavioural problems that children growing up in such settings may display at school or in later life" (*ibid.*, p. 32). This conclusion was echoed in a report by the Commission for Racial Equality in 1988, in which it claimed that some immigrant families found themselves living in conditions far worse than those which they had left, and parents and children were experiencing severe stress and fear. One of the consequences of this pressure on children was behavioural problems at school, which in many instances led to their exclusion (CRE, 1988).

Housing conditions also raised questions about the immigrants' sense of belonging and community. For example, needy families were surprised and distressed to discover that there were Afro-Caribbean people who had acquired property and had become private landlords. These landlords were exploiting the vulnerability of these families, often offering poorly furnished rooms in accommodation where amenities were shared with other tenants while charging exorbitant prices. These conditions frequently led to arguments and made life very stressful and unpleasant. They also undermined a sense of community security, and replaced it with fear, anger, disillusion, and isolation. As expressed to me by one mother, "Everybody was going about his own way and if you die nobody would care". From my own research, and clinical practice, I have found that the fear and mistrust of others has lingered with many of the Afro-Caribbean mothers, restricting their contact with others, their ability to respond to and stimulate their children, and their ability to make friends and find companionship.

In time, some Afro-Caribbean immigrants decided that the solution to their housing difficulties lay in purchasing their own homes. But this solution created new problems. Many of the husbands/ partners were employed in unskilled or semi-skilled jobs. This barely generated enough funds to pay for the mortgage and living expenses. Consequently, mothers of small children then had to seek work to generate additional income. Most of the women, untrained and unskilled, were absorbed into the bottom stream of service jobs with poor wages. Some combined a full-time job during unsociable hours and a part-time job during the day in order to earn enough income to help maintain their families here in the UK and to send remittances to dependents in their home countries. In the absence of an extended family to assist in the care of the children, working full-time caused mothers much stress and anxiety.

In a sample of twenty-three children and their mothers (referred by schools to Child Guidance Clinics), Stewart-Prince, a child psychiatrist, found twenty of the mothers assessed as clinically and seriously depressed. He cited some of the factors contributing to the mothers' depression as "homesickness, feelings of isolation in their neighbourhood, disillusion with the quality of their lives in this country and marital conflict". He also identified some of the mothers who "were struggling with considerable feelings of guilt at having to leave their older children behind" (Stewart-Prince, 1972, p. 106).

Clearly, poor and inadequate housing added to the complexities of the lives of migrant families. In the cramped and confined environment in which they lived, parents (especially mothers) were too often exhausted from managing their living conditions whilst working long hours. These circumstances too often left them with little emotional energy and time to meet adequately their children's emotional and social needs. At least in some communities in the 1970s, black women became active in campaigning for better housing and better housing to provide care for their children (Bryan, Dadzie, & Scafe, 1985).

Today, poor housing, especially in the inner cities, still poses a problem for families, including those of African-Caribbean origins. Living in sub-standard housing affects their physical and mental health and can adversely affect relationships within families. It is important for policy makers to integrate policies for housing, education, and social services in order to treat children and their families holistically.

Childcare

Bowlby argued that if the job of caring for children was to be done well, principal carer(s) needed a great deal of assistance. But the care of children (and their care-givers) was lamentably low on the list of public, governmental priorities, especially in such a society where "man and woman power devoted to the production of material goods counts a plus in all our economic indices". He warned that

> just as a society in which there is a chronic insufficiency of food may take a deplorably inadequate level of nutrition as its norm, so may a society in which parents of young children are left on their own with a chronic insufficiency of help, take this state of affairs as its norm. [Bowlby, 1988, p. 2]

As Pugh noted, "services for children under five in Britain had never been high on the national agenda" (Pugh, 1988, p. 1).

Bowlby's writings on maternal deprivation first appeared in the 1950s, when Britain was recovering from the devastation of the Second World War. Considerable disruption of families had occurred, not only with men going to the front to fight, but with the thousands of children who had been separated from their mothers and families through evacuation. Singer expressed the view that, during post-war reconstruction, Bowlby's theory had gained prominence partly because of the recognition it had given to the importance of family bonds. One slogan of the time was "Restoration of families is restoration of the nation"—a position that also echoed the popular belief that a woman's place was in the home caring for children while the men went out to work (Singer, 1992). Unfortunately, this ideology served the government well as a justification for withdrawing the financial support for crèches and day nurseries which had been provided during the war years.

Indeed, according to Pugh (1988), in 1945 the Minister of Health published a circular purporting to be influenced by the views of Bowlby and Winnicott on the importance of the mother–child bond. The circular claimed that, in the interest of the health and development of the child and for the benefit of the mother, the proper place for a child under two years old was at home with mother. It also declared that, in peace-time, the right policy would be to discourage mothers with children under the age of two from going out to work. The government proposed the provision of nursery schools and nursery classes for children 2–5 years old. Furthermore, day nurseries and day guardians were to be regarded as supplements to meet special needs (Ministry of Health, 1945).

For children of Afro-Caribbean immigrants, these arrangements were particularly significant. Upon arrival in Britain, immigrant families discovered that government agencies paid little or no attention to the fact that they were mainly young and of child-bearing age. And, since the policy in Britain at the time was to encourage mothers to stay at home with their young children, there was little consideration given to the provision of childcare facilities for those women who needed waged work.

In families where both parents needed to work, parents struggled to find ways to provide care for their children. For example, where fathers worked on evening shifts they cared for the children during the day while mothers worked. This arrangement of father as primary care-giver was a departure from the pattern among Caribbean families, where child-care was seen as exclusively the women's task. Then, too, fathers could not always provide the best standard of care after a long night's work; they were exhausted, which diminished their ability to respond to the needs of a young child who was awake and alert during the day. Nevertheless, where fathers were able to actively engage with their children, the bond between father and child was strong.

Some Social Service Departments had a limited number of day care nurseries, but tightened their admission procedures; the criteria for the allocation of a place in nursery had to be financial, social, or medical (Van der Eyken, 1984). The nurseries were seen as doing "preventive" work with families considered to be "at risk". (This judgment, of course, stigmatized the service as well as those seeking it.) At any rate, Afro-Caribbean women who were married or cohabiting with a partner and in full-time employment often did not qualify for the service. Consequently, many of the migrant families turned to child-minders to provide care for their young children. This option, however, had its limitations.

For example, although there was legislation that required child-minders to be registered and their premises to be safe, immigrant families were not sufficiently aware of the processes by which the minder's registration and premises could be checked. Desperate for assistance, they very often accepted questionable premises. As one woman told me,

> I had to go to work and took her [the child] to a child minder. What could I do? I see the oil heater there in the room . . . I know the place is not as it should be, but I had to work to get a place for ourselves, so I just hoped for the best. [Robertson, 1975, p. 9]

In some instances, registered child-minders discriminated against black parents and, according to Ahmed, Cheetham, and Small (1986), many local authorities turned a blind eye to those who discriminated, contending that it would be wrong to impose on child-minders the care of children towards whom they felt awkward or hostile.

There were those families, of course, who had acquired better jobs and could pay the fees to privately run nurseries. However, the idea of their children being looked after by total strangers was barely tolerated, even in the absence of the extended families. Some couples decided that they would prefer to eke out their existence on the sole income of the husband, while the mother would remain at home to care for their children.

Thus, for many Afro-Caribbean families, inadequate child-care provision deepened the stress of settling and surviving in the UK. To these difficult circumstances were added the problems entailed in bringing over children who had been left behind in the Caribbean. Once immigrant parents realized that their stay in the UK would not be temporary, they sent for their children who had been cared for by grandparents and extended families. Immigrant parents had envisaged a reconstituted family—one in which the older children would assume the role of carer for the younger ones; this was the cultural practice mainly among the families of lower socio-economic background.

Mothers had not been prepared for the emotional troubles that those children left behind had had to manage; these children had experienced a double loss, first when their parents left them to migrate to Britain, and again when the children had to leave their care-givers in the Caribbean to join parents in the UK. Then, when children and parents were reunited, they were strangers to each other—occasionally in a family with new siblings—and their relationships were ragged with resentment and mistrust. This often resulted in behaviours by the children that unsettled the parents. Some mothers tried to impose strict discipline, including corporal punishment, but this deepened the child's sense of alienation and anger. Then, too, the children were developing a new cultural identity as they mixed with their British peers.

Confused about the source of their children's distress and the behavioural problems it generated, parents sought out Social Services for assistance. But they did not receive the help that they needed. Social workers were not sufficiently prepared to work with the migrant families and did not understand the cultural backgrounds from which they came. Among other things, social workers were critical of parents who had left their children in the Caribbean. Parents felt that, at best, they were sidelined by social workers; mothers described to me the lack of understanding and unwillingness by some professionals to listen to their problems and involve them in plans to help their children (Robertson, 1975). In many instances, the children were removed from their homes, as social workers assumed they would be better looked after in residential children's homes. There were also mothers who admitted in conversation with me that they were unable to cope with their children's behaviour and had requested that "the Government looked after them" (*ibid.*). How little they understood at the time the effects that these broken attachments would have on their children and themselves and the sense of rejection that the children would carry with them throughout their lives.

Conclusion

The history of Afro-Caribbean immigrants who came to settle in the UK in the post-war period, is a story of unwanted separation and loss. Certainly, the migration experience itself threatened attachments and affectional bonds. But, when the process of settling in and surviving took place in an unwelcoming environment, the sense of dispossession and loss deepened. In addition to hostile—and often conflicting—policies by the UK government, Afro-Caribbean immigrants met with inadequate systems of support to help them meet their perfectly ordinary needs for jobs, decent housing, and the care of their children.

In many respects, the problems of housing and child-care were not unique to black families; much of the British working class and the poor also struggled for decent wages, clean and adequate accommodation, and assistance in balancing the demands of work and child-care. However, migration entailed particular kinds of loss and, when coupled with the experience of racism, the struggle to survive assumed additional burdens. In short, trauma accumulated through loss of home, place, family, identity, self-respect, and esteem.

The inability of successive post-war governments to think beyond their limited economic objectives in seeking labour from the Caribbean created social and emotional problems within and across the generations. I think it is safe to argue that Afro-Caribbean families are still paying the price. In important respects, however, policies that fail to recognize the importance of attachments in the emotional health and development of people and communities are not specific to Afro-Caribbean populations. Rather, they are indicative of societies that, as Bowlby suggested, take as a norm the chronic insufficiency of regard for children.

Currently, the UK government is seeking ways to get more women back into the workplace. While this process can help women to fulfil their economic and social needs, government bodies need to provide assistance for families with young children.

Certainly, good quality child-care must be a high priority. It is also essential for fathers to be more involved with the care of the children and to be given the appropriate support in helping them meet the emotional needs of their children. (The role of fathers in the care of children has received lamentably little attention until recently.)

The caring professions also have a responsibility to help families make and maintain secure attachments. So, for example, where there is family breakdown, professionals need to support kinship care when this is suitable and available; this will help families provide continuity of care, especially within their cultural milieu. Furthermore, resources are needed to train social workers and care workers to recognize attachment disorders among children, and to help families struggling with the trauma of unwanted separation and loss. It is also essential that the relevant statutory bodies develop and monitor attachment-sensitive policies for the benefit of the whole population.

References

Ahmed, A. S., Cheetham, J., & Small, S. J. (1986). *Social Work With Black Children and Their Families*. London: Batsford.

Arnold, E. E. (2001). Broken attachments of women from the West Indies separated from mothers in early childhood. Unpublished PhD Thesis, University of London.

Bonham-Carter, M. (1987). The liberal hour and race relations. *New Community, xiv*(1/2): 1–5.

Bousquet, B., & Douglas, C. (1991). *West Indian Women At War: British Racism in World War II*. London: Lawrence & Wishart.

Bowlby, J. (1952). *Maternal Care and Mental Health*. Geneva: World Health Organization.

Bowlby, J (1969). *Attachment and Loss: Volume 1*. London: Hogarth.

Bowlby, J. (1988). A *Secure Base. Applications of Attachment Clinical Theory*. London: Tavistock/Routledge.

Bryan, B., Dadzie, S., & Scafe, S. (1985). *The Heart of the Race: Black Women's Lives in Britain*. London: Virago.

Commission for Racial Equality (1988). *Living in Terror*. London: CRE.

Freud, A., & Burlingham, D. (1974). *Infants Without Families*. London: Hogarth.

Hood, C., Oppe, T. E., Pless, I. B., & Apte, E. (1970). *Children of West Indian Immigrants: A Study of One-Year-Olds in Paddington.* London: Institute of Race Relations.

Marris, P. (1958). *Loss and Change.* London: Routledge & Kegan Paul.

Ministry of Health (1945). *Nursery Provision for Children Under Five.* Circular 221/45. London: HMSO.

Osborn, A. F., & Butler N. R. (1985). Ethnic minority children: a comparative study from birth to five years. London: Commission for Racial Equality.

Parkes, C. M. (1978). *Bereavement: Studies of Grief in Adult Life.* Harmondsworth: Penguin.

Peach, C. (1968). *West Indian Migration to Britain: A Social Geography.* London: Institute of Race Relations, & Oxford University Press.

Pugh, G. (1988). *Services For Under Fives: Developing a Coordinated Approach.* London: National Children's Bureau.

Robertson, E. E. (1975). Out of sight, not out of mind. Unpublished MPhil Thesis, University of Sussex.

Robertson, J. (1969). *A Two-Year Old Goes to Hospital* (film). London: Tavistock Child Development Research Unit.

Singer, E. (1992). *Childcare and the Psychology of Development.* London: Routledge.

Stewart-Prince, G. (1972). Mental health problems in pre-school West Indian children. In: J. P. Triseliotis (Ed.), *Social Work with Coloured Immigrants and Their Families* (pp. 102–108). London: Oxford University Press.

Van der Eyken, (1984). *Day Nurseries in Action: a National Study of Local Authority Day Nurseries in England 1975–1983.* Final report. Department of Child Health Research Unit: University of Bristol.

CHAPTER FIVE

Seeking asylum: the struggle for a new secure base

Chris Purnell and Katharine Shubinsky

For a few moments, think about how your day started today. When you left home this morning, maybe you took your children to school, said hurried goodbyes to your partner or loved ones. Perhaps you were thinking about the day ahead of you, and everything that you had to do today as you travelled to your destination, or maybe your mind was focused upon something that you had planned for this evening.

Whatever your particular circumstances, it is likely to involve all sorts of assumed expectations about continuity and routine in your life.

Now, thinking about your particular journey or routine, imagine how you might feel if you were stopped by the authorities on the way to your destination. No reason is given for your detention, but you are detained indefinitely.

You are frightened and confused. You do not know what is going to happen to you. The only certainty that you now have is that you will not be allowed to return home, and your life as you know it, along with the people who are part of it, are gone.

The only thing that you have left is uncertainty . . .

How would you feel?

John Bowlby (1988) wrote about the importance of a secure base as part of an attachment system that provides human beings with protection and comfort at times of actual or threatened danger, illness, or fatigue. He conceived of the secure base in the form of another human being, but it is also the case that comfort and a sense of safety can be derived from a familiar environment. The brief scenario just described reflects the experience of many refugees and asylum seekers who have been forcibly separated from not only their families and loved ones, but also their social networks. In their separation, they have lost the secure base that those people and communities provided.

What we will consider in this chapter are the experiences of some of our clients who have sought asylum, and our experiences of working to help them in overcoming their traumas. Although the term "asylum seeker" is used for the sake of brevity, much of what we refer to is also applies to our clients who are refugees.

A hostile environment

The Taliban killed Ali's father, mother, and brother. He hid in the house of a neighbour for safety and watched as they were shot. Later, he fled into the mountains and made a perilous journey to safety in a neighbouring country, where an uncle had arranged and paid for him to be transported to the West. As he climbed into the back of the lorry he had no way of knowing which country he was being taken to. It was not until he arrived in Dover and asked for asylum that he knew that England was to be his destination.

Like so many asylum seekers, Ali suffered overwhelming loss and he carried his loss with him as he entered the UK. Sadly, what he—like others—was to discover was that he arrived in a country with little sympathy for his plight. It is worth reflecting on the kind of social environment to which asylum seekers come, because it too often deepens the trauma they have already experienced.

Much of that environment is confusing. Having to negotiate the rules and regulations of entry to the UK is considerably difficult, as is finding one's way around in unfamiliar towns where temporary accommodation has been provided. The lack of social and emotional support while making one's way through an unfamiliar social system can deepen an already existing sense of unease and fear caused by previous trauma. What most citizens can take for granted in the routines of their daily lives become the extraordinary obstacles that asylum seekers must negotiate.

The environment is often experienced as hostile. Government policy on immigration has contributed to elements of racism and nationalism within British culture that have shaped recent media images of those seeking asylum. Represented as threats to the "British national identity", and as unworthy foreign competitors for economic and social resources, asylum seekers are often portrayed as desperate "economic migrants", who will risk life and limb just to improve their standards of living. The desperation, of course, is real, but the underlying traumatic causes are less frequently exposed on television or in the press. The danger is that stories such as Ali's journey to survive remain concealed from public view and can barely be heard through the noise of media distortion.

The interplay between "public opinion" and government policy contributes to a hostile social climate, which in turn shapes the way social institutions treat asylum seekers. In the case of social support structures, for example, service provision can be uneven and entitlement unclear. Within public services, which are struggling to cope with huge demands for limited resources, the needs of asylum seekers are perceived as additional and unwelcome demands. In a country where political agendas dictate that service cost savings and efficiency are paramount, asylum seekers are not a priority— they rarely constitute core business that will attract funding. Furthermore, for individuals who are in the front line and trying to provide services under these pressured conditions, there is often also compassion fatigue, resulting in asylum seekers receiving only minimal support and very little understanding. Consequently, the perception (and experience) of many asylum seekers whom we see is that staff who deal with them are at best uncompassionate and at worst racist in their responses towards them.

As asylum moves up the political agenda, so the process of reaching a point of safety by being given leave to remain by the Home Office becomes increasingly difficult. Many people have waited for years for a decision, with no secure base to turn to for safety or reassurance. As one asylum seeker put it: "I thought that when I got to the UK I was safe, but my troubles began when I arrived here . . . still, three years on, I am not safe. I do not know if they will send me back."

The absence of a secure base, and the hopelessness and despair that a hostile environment can generate, can lead to additional problems. Asylum seekers awaiting a decision about their claims have no home. They are moved to new temporary accommodation on a regular basis. They have no right to work, and in some circumstances must use vouchers rather than money to buy food. It is no wonder that their mental health can be at risk.

When we first started working with this client group, the most consistent feedback that we received was about our "kindness". To begin with, this came as something of a surprise. We did not treat asylum seekers any differently to any other of our clients, so why should they remark about our kindness? Kindness was just something that we took for granted as part of providing a caring service. The significance of this feedback only became apparent as we became more familiar with the hostile environment that asylum seekers have to contend with on a day-to-day basis.

For those who have endured imprisonment, torture, interrogation, and the loss of loved ones in their home country, there are often also physical and mental health difficulties to contend with. These are the people that we tend to see for psychotherapeutic treatment. For many, the psychotherapy group that we started became their secure base. It was not just the relationships that developed with us as therapists that were important; it was also the relationships that that they developed with the group. For some, the group has become their new family, the place where new attachments can begin to grow and develop.

Creating safety

Herman (1992) identifies three stages to the process of recovery from complex trauma such as that experienced by many asylum seekers, and this is the model that we use for the psychotherapy group. Given that danger of one sort or another has been a significant part of the traumatizing experience, creating safety is the first requirement for recovery. This is the recreation of a secure base. The second part of the process is to be able to mourn the losses relating to the trauma. Bowlby (1991) himself regarded mourning as the natural way of healing loss; a process through which we are able to begin to let go of what we have lost and move on. This relates to Herman's third stage of recovery, which is reconnection. For asylum seekers, this involves finding new connections with individuals from sometimes different cultural and ethnic backgrounds, and ultimately with a social environment that has been previously experienced as hostile.

When human beings are feeling unsafe, they will, as Bowlby described, respond with attachment-related behaviour. If they have previous experience of secure attachments, then they will readily seek safety and comfort from others who are able to protect them until the danger passes. Secure attachment involves the experiencing of a protective responsiveness on the part of care-givers in situations that are perceived as threatening or dangerous. However, if their past attachments have not been secure, individuals will not necessarily seek safety in this way. Their strategy may be overly self reliant—because this is how they have previously learnt to deal with danger with attachment figures who were not protective. This self-reliance can be problematic, as it limits an individual's ability to seek and accept much-needed help, support, and comfort. They might, on the other hand, be very preoccupied with potential danger and not readily reassured about safety, because the protection provided by previous attachment figures has been inconsistent and unpredictable.

This is true of asylum seekers, but there is often the additional complication of trauma caused by torture and ill-treatment and the sudden and sometimes violent loss of previous attachment relationships. The threat of danger produces increased levels of arousal that lead initially to safety- and comfort-seeking, but if the danger continues and there is no one who can provide the required safety, then the intensity of arousal level increases to anger and fear as the self-protective strategies employed increase in response to the uncontained threat or danger (Crittenden, 2000). Prolonged and extreme trauma influences the ability to regulate affect—to control and manage feelings appropriately. This leaves asylum seekers with difficulties, for example, in containing angry feelings, or with problems of hyper-vigilance and anxiety. With these raised levels of arousal, concentration and memory also become a problem.

The social difficulties that can arise because of these problems can be multiple. Frustration easily boils over into anger and aggression when faced with the perceived unresponsiveness and rejection of public services that are supposed to provide help and support, or, in other words, safety. Thus, the situation can arise where even the organizations that are available to provide support and help to asylum seekers and refugees can withdraw their services from the person whose anger and aggression are too much for the organization to contain.

Similarly, regulating anger can become a problem for the person with a family with young children, whose crying or laughter creates an intolerable noise:

> when Sead's baby cries, the sound reminds him of the screams of the hundreds of people who were killed when his town was bombed.

The only way for some to deal with this is to withdraw into the safety and isolation of another room, away from the sounds of daily family life. This in itself has implications for the attachment relationship with the children and increases the potential for the transgenerational transmission of anxious attachments. There is also the potential for domestic violence within asylum-seeker families, as individuals who have endured traumatic experiences of violence and torture often have difficulty in their day-to-day management of anger.

Problems with memory and concentration are also common.

> Yousaf frequently loses items such as mobile phones and umbrellas, which he puts down in shops and then forgets to pick up when he leaves. When he is at home he often forgets to check on food that he has left cooking on the stove and burnt saucepans are common. On a recent occasion he returned home and found that he couldn't open his front door. It was only when a neighbour challenged him that he realized that he was trying to open the front door of the wrong house.

There are potential dangers arising out these sorts of situations, with the risk of fire being an obvious concern. However, in this particular instance the potential for misunderstanding Yousaf's intentions when he tried to get into the wrong house could have been quite serious, particularly if there had been a general mistrust and suspicion of asylum seekers in the community.

Flashbacks and nightmares are very common. When you have been taken from your home or off the street and have experienced the total power of your persecutors over whether you live or die, it is not easy to then simply accept that you are now safe. You lock your doors and windows at all times, and at night you sleep with the light on. As one asylum seeker put it, "my nightmares began when I knew that I was safe". For some, sleepwalking may be a problem:

> Ahmed sometimes wakes in the night and finds himself standing in the street in his night clothes, in a very unsafe area of the town where he lives.

Sometimes lives have been so completely shattered that it is difficult to begin to put the pieces together again.

> Ibrahim was a high ranking army officer in his home country until his son was arrested and tortured. Ibrahim tried to intervene and was himself arrested and tortured, as was his wife. He escaped from prison by paying a bribe and eventually arrived in the UK, where his asylum request was refused and he was left homeless and without support. Some of his younger fellow countrymen took him in because he reminded them of their own fathers from whom they were separated. Between them they made sure that he was cared for. Ibrahim has frequently been found in a very confused state wandering the streets, searching for his family. The young men who care for him pin a label to his clothes, giving his name and address so that he can be returned safely to them when he wanders off.

For some asylum seekers, depression and a sense of hopelessness is the overwhelming experience. Very often this is related to the loss of attachments.

> Yasamen is an only child. When she was forced to flee from her home and country, she left behind her ageing father, who is unwell. After more than three years of waiting, she was given leave to remain in the UK, but the joy of finally finding safety was overshadowed by the pain of separation from her father. At times her pain has been so great that she has begged us to help her to return home so that she can be with her father, even though it would mean certain imprisonment and probably torture and death. Complying with her request for help would be tantamount to assisting her to commit suicide.

In some instances, asylum seekers whom we see have been persecuted in their own country because of their sexuality. Owing to cultural and religious taboos, they are at risk of isolation and rejection within their own small communities in the UK if they reveal their sexuality. It remains a carefully concealed secret that they carry with them, and they can never feel completely safe because of it. The secret means that they have to create a different story to explain to their community why it was that they had to leave their home country. Sometimes this may involve having to create a fictitious partner and children that they have left behind, and the more elaborate the story becomes, the harder it also is to maintain.

These are just some of the issues that asylum seekers face that relate to safety and the need to feel safe. While attempting to address some of the individual needs with one-to-one therapy, we also offer a secure base in the form of a therapy group. For many people, this has become just that; a place where they know that they can come every week and get emotional sustenance from others who have had their own particular traumas and difficulties. It is a group with diverse languages, but no interpreters are used. Instead, we rely on language dictionaries and each other to create a common understanding using English. This is a crucially important aspect of the recovery model that we use in that it encourages sharing and moving from individual isolation to reconnection with others who are also trying to rebuild their lives in the UK.

The group therapy offered differs from the more conventional psychodynamic model in that we sometimes incorporate drinking tea or eating food into a session. Part of the rationale for this is that food and drink are comforting, and comfort-seeking is a natural part of attachment behaviour. The group provides a more nurturing secure base with the inclusion of these rituals, which can also be about the celebration of achievements, successes, or anniversaries. The other reason why we do this has to do with reconnection, and the sharing of the diversity of customs and beliefs that the group members have, and that can co-exist. This sharing and respect for others also extends to the healing of some emotional wounds, as the Bosnian survivor of violence and oppression in a Serb concentration camp finds ways to connect with the Eritrean veteran soldier who has perpetrated violence and might also have been an oppressor.

Nature's cure

John Bowlby (1988) considered mourning, which involves the expression of distress and anger, to be part of a natural response to loss of attachment. The signalling of distress and anger are the means by which we as human beings attempt to recover threatened or lost attachment bonds. Furthermore, when attachments are irrevocably lost, mourning is the natural way of adjusting to the loss. Thus, much of the group process is focused upon the mourning of loss. Mourning provides the bridge between achieving safety and the ability to then reconnect with the world.

The mood within the group can fluctuate very quickly as individuals share their experiences and then withdraw into reflective silence as they regulate the emotions that the telling of their story has stirred up.

All stages of the mourning process are alive in the group. Sometimes we hear about people searching for family members with whom they have lost touch when they had to flee their homes under circumstances already described.

We listen to idealizations of a way of life that has been lost forever because of wars or the annihilation of whole communities. We hear about summertimes in Bosnia, when the sun shone and life was simple and without worries; a time when it was possible to walk the streets in complete safety and food was plentiful, and, because it was organic, it tasted so much better than what is available in a UK supermarket. This is not simply an idyllic view of the past; it is an important part of the process of mourning where people remember and reminisce about a way of life that has been lost.

We also hear about the guilt and shame that is left as a residue of having succumbed to torture.

Redzo was told by a guard to kick another prisoner who was already being beaten. He knew that if he did not obey then he could be killed, and yet he had never been a violent man. He complied with the guard's demand and kicked his fellow prisoner, but he kicked him very gently. Redzo still lives with the guilt of his own violence.

We can only speculate as to whether Redzo's attachment style helped him to survive in the concentration camp. Given that strategies for attachment develop from learned responses to events in the past that were perceived to be dangerous (Crittenden, 2000), it could be argued that, in some instances, the person who has learned to deal with more dangers in their earlier life because of unreliable attachments might be better equipped strategically to deal with trauma generally (even if it involves re-enacting it) than someone who had a less dangerous experience simply because their attachments were more secure. There are questions that arise about Redzo's torturers; to what extent did their capacity to inflict pain upon others arise out of their own experiences of attachment? It could be that Redzo's guilt arises out of a conflict between his previous experiences of a gentle kind of attachment and care-giving and the need to deal with an imminent threat to his life, which could not be responded to by the use of this familiar strategy. Redzo kicked his fellow prisoner gently, but he risked his own life in doing so.

Sometimes guilt and shame are felt on behalf of a whole community or nation.

Tarik spoke in the group and explained about the history of wars and violence between ethnic groups, warlords, with the Russians and the Taliban in Afghanistan. Tarik has lost all of his family because of the conflicts, but his greatest sadness and shame is for his country because of the unending conflict with seems unresolvable.

If the shame that Tarik feels for his country is a common experience, it raises questions about the extent to which this feeling, and the violence and conflict that have generated it, becomes internalized as part of a nation's psyche and how it then influences attachments at a community level and within families. Psychoanalyst and writer Alice Miller (1987) has written extensively on this theme. Although her writings are focused upon western cultures, she essentially argues that the transmission of cruelty and violence in societies is influenced by practices in child-rearing that have been supported and condoned by society generally for the child's "own good". Thus, what is internalized within the psyche of a nation has a profound affect upon how families bring up their children and upon attachments at not only a family level but also within the community. The past and present foreign policies of various countries that have involved themselves in Afghanistan, and are currently involved (to use Miller's words) "for its own good", have had significant influence upon the current situation that Tarik now internalizes as his own shame.

In our therapy group, we found that the expression of anger and distress was often inhibited, even though in some instances it could be expressed in the safer environment of home. If anger and distress feel dangerous, it is usually because of a fear that such emotions will in some way overwhelm the listener, in much the same way that the expression of distress can be inhibited in attachment relationships because an attachment figure is dismissing or unresponsive to it. In the group, the feeling of being overwhelmed by one's own emotions is projected on to others, who are then perceived as unable to bear the pain and must therefore be protected from it. It was necessary for us as therapists to help the group to feel safe with these difficult feelings, so that they could be expressed more openly as part of the process of mourning.

Mourning losses can also include telling stories about life before the trauma of forced separation and torture. It can involve stories of the loss of identity, of being reduced from the role of the strong breadwinner and protector by abuse and torture, which has left just a shell of the former person. Feeling psychologically and physically weak and dependent can stir up further feelings of helplessness and hopelessness relating to the loss of a clear role or purpose in life.

> Mirza talks about his former life as a breadwinner, working on the oil pipelines in Russia in temperatures that were so cold that all of the men drank vodka for breakfast in order to just keep warm. He talks with pride about the hardships that he endured to earn a good living for his family. As he talks to the group he walks around the room to alleviate the constant physical pain in his body that is a legacy of torture. These days, Mirza's wife and children support him—he is no longer the man that he was.

Many asylum seekers whom we see also have sexual difficulties caused by trauma, depression, medication, or physical pain. Some may have experienced sexual abuse as a form of torture. Sexual relationships are intimately bound with adult attachments, and the loss of sexual functioning can have a huge impact upon individuals and their ability to maintain their closest attachment relationships. Sexual relationships often represent their nearest experience to a secure base.

Many people come from cultures where manhood and sexual functioning are closely linked, and the inability to fulfil this aspect of close relationships results in humiliation, shame, and suicidal thoughts. Similarly, women who were raped in prison sometimes keep this a secret, because of the shame it brings and the fear, or sometimes certain knowledge, that their husband will disown them if it becomes known.

These are just some of the issues relating to loss and mourning that are part of the mix of the emotional life of the group, and the mood of the group fluctuates accordingly with individuals participating and then withdrawing into quiet reflection as they regulate their emotions. There is a fine balance between hope and despair for many people, with a need to express feelings of despair without losing hope and to express hope without dismissing despair. The regulating function of individuals and of the group itself enables this balance to be achieved.

Connecting with others

Telling one's story is an important part of the mourning process, and it is a very important part of the process of being able to move on, but there is also a need to repair the disrupted or broken connection between the individual and others. For asylum seekers, we suggest that there are two dimensions to this task. The first is to help people to heal from their particular trauma and to reconnect, and the second is to help to facilitate a social environment where healing can take place; this is the purpose of the group therapy. However, there is the additional dimension of the communities in which people live, and it is in this area where much still needs to be done.

Social policy and political decisions profoundly influence an asylum seeker's ability to form new secure attachments to individuals and to their new community. Responses to attachment needs should be offered promptly to avoid compounding existing distress and trauma (Bowlby, 1988).

> Muhammed has been waiting for six years for a decision about his asylum claim. To use his own words, the waiting is "killing him".

A speedier judicial process would offer certainty and allow individuals to move on in their lives, because, if granted leave to remain, they are then enabled to work, travel, and fully participate in society.

Housing is a particular need for asylum seekers. Policy for managing housing while they are awaiting a decision regarding their asylum claim results in many asylum seekers being subjected to sudden moves to new accommodation. Sometimes, this is to a different town, where they then have to start to try to rebuild their network of contacts, which can further traumatize and repeat an experience of severed attachments. This disruption impedes the development of new attachment relationships with people and the community, and often interrupts medical and therapeutic care. The provision of safe, quiet, and permanent housing helps to provide a secure base and allows the individual to develop new relationships and networks.

The development of secure attachments is also fostered by the provision of a benign, rather than a frightening or punitive, environment. We can all do something to help create this environment.

> Huso talks about how the goodwill and helpfulness of his neighbour contributed to his adjustment to life in a new community in the UK, when his family were reunited after the Bosnian war. The kindness that he was shown helped to foster a sense of safety and a secure base for the whole family.

Changes in public opinion about the nature of asylum seekers would also aid this process. The asylum seekers with whom we work are not "scroungers", "helpless victims", or "criminals". Some were persecuted for actively campaigning for justice and human rights and against oppression in their home countries. Others are innocent individuals caught up in war or the brutality of totalitarian regimes, or they have been terrorized, tortured, and persecuted simply because of who they are in terms of ethnicity, gender, or sexuality. These are people who have endured enormous loss. However, rather than exist on handouts, they are keen to contribute to society through work and to make the UK their home.

> Huso survived the brutality of two years in concentration camps, and he cherishes the freedoms that his new country offers. The date that he was released from the camps has become day that he celebrates his "birthday"; the day that he found new hope and his life began. He is immensely proud of his British citizenship and his right to vote.

In our experience, it is often the Home Office that has the least empathy or understanding of the plight of many asylum seekers. Even when someone has been granted leave to remain in the UK, they can still experience problems.

> Cesa had news of a sudden family bereavement in his home country and applied to the Home Office for travel documents so that he could travel to a safe nearby country to meet with his family and grieve. His application was refused on the basis that he had not shown any evidence that he had made efforts to approach the Embassy of his home country to apply for a passport and been unable to obtain one. For Cesa to reveal his current whereabouts through contact with the Embassy would involve huge risks to his family, as they are regularly visited by the authorities who are still searching for him. Although the Home Office accepted that the situation in his home country was too dangerous for him to return, there was no recognition of the danger posed to his family if his whereabouts became known to the authorities as a result of his application for a passport.

There is much that could be done through the provision of training for service providers in order that they might help to create a benign environment for this client group. General awareness training of many of the issues that we have described through our experiences of asylum seekers would contribute to an improvement in the way that services are delivered.

An asylum seeker with poor memory and concentration learns better when his English language teacher understands and is empathic with his problems with learning. Similarly, an asylum seeker will be more able to engage with the housing official who understands that fear may present as anger in a housing interview, or a hostel worker might be better equipped to support an asylum seeker resident if they understand the impact that a noisy hostel environment can have upon someone who is suffering from post traumatic stress disorder.

A doctor who demonstrates that they understand the enormity of the fear and shame of an asylum-seeker patient will enable the patient to talk to them more readily about her problems. Asylum seekers are enabled to accurately tell their story in court when the interpreter used not only speaks the same first language, but is also from their own ethnic group and is not a member of the group that oppressed them. This is essential if they are to have a fair hearing before decisions are taken that will profoundly influence their future.

These are a few of the things that can help to make a difference to the experiences of people who have suffered attachment traumas and losses that most of us would find hard to imagine. Indeed, this is possibly one reason why our society's response is generally hostile, because we are confronted with the potential fragility of our own social systems and social institutions when we become aware of the threats to basic human dignity and survival such as those experienced by asylum seekers. Meeting the asylum seeker as a human being brings their trauma, with all of its horrors, into sharp focus, and stirs within us with our own personal fears and prejudices.

People seeking asylum have the right to be treated with dignity, respect, and kindness. Consistently, the fundamental plea to society that we hear from the people whom we see is simply to be treated like a human being. Responding to this basic need will aid recovery and foster the development of secure attachments. It will also minimize the potential for the transgenerational transmission of anxious attachments. Furthermore, it will enhance the dignity of the community and promote social cohesion—something that has benefits for us all.

References

Bowlby, J. (1988). *A Secure Base. Clinical Applications of Attachment Theory*. London: Tavistock/Routledge.

Bowlby, J. (1991). *Attachment and Loss Vol.3. Loss, Sadness and Depression*. London: Penguin.

Crittenden, P. M. (2000). Dynamic–maturational exploration of the meaning of security and adaptation. In: P. M. Clausen & A. H. Clausen (Eds.), *The Organisation of Attachment Relationships: Maturation, Culture and Context* (pp. 00–00). Cambridge: Cambridge University Press.

Herman, J. L. (1992). *Trauma and Recovery: The Aftermath of Violence—From Domestic Abuse to Political Terror*. New York: Basic Books.

Miller, A. (1987). *For Your Own Good: The Roots of Violence in Child-rearing*. London: Virago.

CHAPTER SIX

Compassion deficit disorder? The impact of consuming culture on children's relationships

Diane Levin

Introduction

Imagine the following three responses to babies in distress. (Throughout this chapter, the gender of the child in the stories is used as it was reported. However, in the commentary, "he" and "she" is used interchangeably, unless otherwise indicated.)

A baby is crying in his crib. His father comes in and begins talking to him and gently patting his back. As the crying continues, the father picks up the baby and hugs and cuddles him. Each time the baby lets out a yelp, his father rubs his back and then begins to sing a soothing song. The baby gradually calms down and, as the singing continues, he begins to watch his father's face and smile.

The second baby is crying in her crib. In the course of flailing her arms and legs, her big toe seems to end up in her mouth almost by chance. She pauses as she focuses on what has just happened. Her crying slows and then stops as she begins sucking her toe in earnest.

The third baby also begins to cry in her crib. Her mother quickly enters the room and pushes a button on the electronic crib toy that the family received as a baby gift. Lights begin to flash and music plays. As soon as the lights start flashing, the baby turns to the lights, stops crying and becomes completely still, as if in a daze.

What's going on in these three situations? How are they the same, how are they different, and why do the differences matter? And how does what is happening relate to the development of attachments and other relational bonds in the lives of today's children?

In all three scenarios, we see a baby in distress. In all three we also see some new factor intervening in a way that enables the baby to calm down. If our goal is to help babies stop crying when they are distressed, then all three situations effectively meet our goal. But does this mean that all three approaches are equally positive ways to meet babies' needs when they cry? I would argue "no", definitely not.

In the first situation, the father serves as the comforter of the baby. As he and his baby interact, the give and take that occurs between them ultimately leads to a contented baby and parent. Each response of the baby leads to a reaction from the father, so that baby and father have a mutual exchange. The baby and adult are developing a unique, mutual way of interacting. The baby comes to associate his father's responsive physical contact, language, and singing with a positive connection with another person and a sense of well-being and safety—exactly what is at the core of secure attachment. The baby gradually learns to accommodate his own behaviour to the familiar responses of his father. He also learns the satisfaction and sense of power that comes from experiencing a reciprocal relationship. Repeated experiences like this, with predictable and caring adults, lay the foundation for positive and secure attachment relationships with significant others. This foundation will influence the nature of intimate relationships throughout life. It will also help children to learn the appropriate behaviour required to successfully engage in everyday reciprocal interactions with others (Bowlby, 1969).

In the second situation, when the baby chews on her toes, she actually succeeds in comforting herself. Learning to self-comfort—to *self-soothe*—is a gradual and essential process that will help her to develop a sense of competence and skill in her own abilities. (Of course, this does not happen independently of the experiences of attachment that the infant will accumulate.) The discovery helps her stop crying as she tries out her newly-found skill. The next time she is upset, she has a resource available to help herself feel better, and she can do it all by herself. Over time, this baby may learn that when she is upset, she has within her own power something she can do to provide self-soothing. She is also learning *self-regulation*—how to control herself and her behaviour, and, in so doing, how to have a positive effect on herself and her world as she comes to understand her ability to influence both objects and other people (White, 1959).

In the third situation, still other forces are at work. The bells and whistles of the crib toy seem to startle the baby into silence. Young children are naturally drawn to the salient and dramatic stimuli that toys such as this one offer. Every time the button is pushed, the bells and whistles grab the baby's attention without her doing anything more than turning her head. The toy does not provide the give and take interaction with either another person or with herself. She does not have the opportunity to understand the cause and effect her direct actions play in the comforting process. This "push-button" approach to soothing makes this baby the passive recipient of a quick fix that actually can undermine what she learns about how to connect with others in a mutually rewarding way (Levin & Rosenquest, 2001).

Children need many opportunities to build an increasingly sophisticated repertoire of actions they can use to influence their social world; these are represented in the first two situations. In the third situation, however, the bells and whistles of the push-button toy deprive the baby of chances to develop the motivation and skills for connecting with self or others. The description on the package in which the push-button toy came promised that it would lead to a soothed and contented baby. What parent would not want that for their child? But, in reality, the toy runs the risk of doing just the opposite.

Commercial culture and the "quick fix, throw away" approach to life

Unfortunately, today's commercial culture is producing too many experiences for babies and children of the kind we see in the third example. Vast sums of money are spent every year selling products to children and their parents. The products are usually created to make money, not necessarily to promote the well-being of children (Linn, 2005; Schor, 2005). And many of these products, as well as the techniques used for marketing them, encourage children towards a push-button, quick fix approach to their relationships and to life.

Childhood has not always been shaped in these ways. In the USA, massive marketing efforts were not directed at children until the mid 1980s, when the Federal Communications Commission deregulated children's television. Deregulation made it possible for the television and toy industries to work together to create whole lines of products (such as bedsheets, pyjamas, breakfast cereals, and lunch-boxes) that were linked to children's television programmes and other media. It was at this time that young children began to be targeted as a distinctive consumer group, and television marketing for this new niche became highly profitable. Within one year of deregulation, eight of the best-selling toys were linked to television shows (Levin, 1998). Soon afterwards new programmes like *Transformers*, *Care Bears*, *My Little Pony*, *Teenage Mutant Ninja Turtles*, and the *Mighty Morphin Power Rangers* joined the market mania. Such marketing practices then quickly spread beyond the USA.

With deregulation, media and marketing directed at children became a much bigger force in children's lives, quickly touching almost everything they do from the time they wake up in the morning until they go to bed at night. The average child in the USA now spends more time in front of the screen than in doing anything else except sleeping (Roberts, Foehr, & Rideout, 2005). One third of children aged zero to six years have a television set in their bedroom (Rideout, Vandewater, & Wartella, 2003).

Media culture has changed childhood in two fundamental ways. First, it has affected *how* children interact in the world. Second, the actual content of the programming children see has influenced the lessons they learn about the nature of relationships and how people treat each other.

Loss of internal control and mastery

The media and commercial cultures make children's interactions with objects and people more rote and programmed (Levin, 1998).

The process starts in the crib with push-button toys and other elec-tronic products for babies, such as Baby Einstein and Leap Frog products, and Sesame Beginnings videotapes recommended by the manufacturers for babies three months old or younger. As infants become children, they are exposed to new marketing initiatives through age-related television programmes, movies, DVDs, com-puters, video games and other electronics.

Often, it is these objects and the visual media that control chil-dren, as children become less in charge of themselves. When chil-dren are glued to a screen, they are engaged in someone else's agenda. Media-linked toys often channel children into *imitating* what they see on the screen rather than *creating* their own play, activities, or ideas. Many toys can do only *one thing in one way* and cannot change and evolve with the child's ideas or skills. Soon, children are looking for the next new object that will give them the next new fix, because the old toy has become boring (Levin, 2007).

Acquiring a new object can be like the child's first drug, as get-ting it becomes equated with happiness in children's minds. But this is not the kind of happiness or personal satisfaction that comes from accomplishing something on one's own. The drive to acquire objects to feel happy contributes to a "throw away" approach to objects, and, perhaps, even to relationships with others. In sum, commercial culture is profoundly changing how children interact with the world and the nature of their relationships with objects and people.

Harmful messages

The media and commercial cultures also influence the quality of children's relationships through the content of the objects children consume; that is, the media help to shape the lessons children learn about what is expected and desirable in the way people treat each other. For instance, the exercise of violence and power toward others is often portrayed as the preferred way to solve conflicts. Toys marketed through the media encourage children to imitate in their play the antisocial behaviour they see on the screen, a process that amplifies the power of the messages the media deliver (Levin & Carlsson-Paige, 2006).

Media and commercial cultures also teach children lessons about identity, especially what it means to be a boy and a girl. For example, violence is a favourite strategy used to sell products to boys, and in the twenty years since deregulation there has been an enormous increase in violent media and products. There have also been numerous blockbuster violent television programmes that market whole lines of items connected to that violence. When a recent *Star Wars* movie—rated PG-13 because of the violence it contained—was released, over a thousand products were on sale with the Starwar's logo. Most of these products contained images of violence.

Among the lessons boys learn from this violence is that boys are supposed to be tough, ready to fight, and utterly self-reliant. But being a tough guy can cut off boys from the feelings of empathy for others that they need in order to have mutually empowering relationships. "Hurt—don't help" is a message that permeates our culture of masculinity.

Appearance and sexual appeal, on the other hand, are marketed to girls (Levin & Kilbourne, in preparation). The enormously popular Bratz dolls—with their highly sexualized bodies, clothes, jewellery, and make-up—surpassed the sales of the Barbie doll line by the end of 2006. Bratz dolls now have their own TV show and a clothing line that includes a matching padded bra and bikini pants set for girls as young as four years old. Girls quickly learn to see themselves and others as *objects*; how they look and what they can buy becomes the basis of their self-understanding and social judgements. In addition, as the model of the ideal self has become one with a dangerously thin body, more and more girls can develop unhealthy relationships with their objectified bodies in their efforts to meet the ideal.

The toll of commercial culture on children and beyond

Understanding how children learn and develop helps us to appreciate the impact of commercial culture on their emerging sense of self and capacities for relationships. Children gradually build ideas about themselves and others from their direct experiences. They connect new experiences to what they already know, and adapt what they know to make sense of the new things that happen. Children do not understand their experience as adults do, as their age, level of development, and prior experiences all affect the meanings they make. For instance, young children's thinking is more like a slide than a movie; they do not easily make logical causal connections between events or ideas. They tend to be ego-centric, so they relate experiences to themselves and have a hard time taking into account another person's point of view.

The following examples, all shared with me by concerned parents and professionals, shed a powerful light on the connection between what is in the media and commercial culture and how children think. They raise disturbing questions about the harm caused by commercial culture on children's relational behaviour.

Remote control childhood?

Recently, a colleague told me that she saw something in a restaurant that worried her a great deal. A young child (about three years old) arrived at a large dinner table with four adults who looked like parents and grandparents. As soon as the child sat down, she started to fidget. Her father quickly whipped out a battery-operated DVD player, put it in front of her, and started a Disney movie. The child stopped fidgeting and became glued to the screen. Her father chuckled to the adult next to him, "That's the only way we'll get any peace!" My colleague concluded, "How sad . . . this kid was totally removed from the conversation of her family or anything else that was going on in the room."

Over the years, children have been spending increasing amounts of time plugged into screens of one kind of another: at home, in airports, on aeroplanes, and in cars; at these moments, they are cut off from the socially engaged give and take, cause and effect, direct experiences they need to learn how to interact in their world.

It even happens at school! A kindergarten teacher who tried to build curriculum activities around the interests of her children decided to pick up on their constant references to involvement with television at home. She helped the children make a "TV set" for the classroom's dramatic play area, using a large cardboard carton. She had hoped to turn the set into an opportunity for the children to do story-telling, perhaps by drawing pictures to show on the screen and making puppets to use to dramatize their stories. But, after completing the TV set, the children went into the dramatic play area, sat on the couch in front of the TV, stared at the hole in the box and refused to budge. What could have provided a rich opportunity for socio-dramatic play, with a lot of valuable role taking and interaction among the children, became just another *remote-controlled* activity.

In the past, children had more opportunities for social interactions through which they could the feel and observe the effects of their behaviour on others and elicit the reactions they desired. Now, however, children are encouraged to be more passive, and are less able to initiate and direct the course of their social exchanges (Levin, 1998).

Problem-solving deficit disorder?

I was visiting a preschool classroom near the beginning of a school year. The teacher enthusiastically put play dough out on a small table. A child sat down, poked and squeezed the play dough a few times, and quickly left the table. Then another child came over, poked it, and asked, "What does it do?" I was startled to see this exchange between the children and the play dough. When I began as a teacher of young children many years ago, play dough was a favourite material for both the children and me. It offered endless possibilities for play that could grow and evolve in relation to the age, stage, experience, and interests of each child. Now, when I describe to other teachers the bored or puzzled reactions to play dough I have observed, many nod knowingly and say that they encounter more and more children who have trouble engaging with this kind of material. Teachers frequently add that even when children do get involved, they often quickly end up having conflicts with other children about how to share. Seeing these children's responses made me worry about how they were missing out on so many of the social, emotional, and cognitive learning opportunities creative play can provide.

Have they come to expect electronic screens, toys, and play materials to show them what to do? Are they unable to see new materials and situations as providing interesting new *problems* to solve, such as: "What happens when I mash it down really hard? Wow! I made a pancake." And, if children have difficulty working on the problems a new material presents, what will they be like when they encounter a problem or conflict with other children? Will they be more likely to use aggression to solve problems, in the manner they see on television? Will they be able to find solutions to problems in ways that they can work out, productively, for themselves?

I have come to use the term *problem-solving deficit disorder* (PSDD) (Levin, in press; Meltz, 2004) to describe the behaviour exemplified by the children who do not know what to do with objects (like play dough) or their conflicts with others. Children with PSDD have a hard time being the active agents of their involvement with the world. The concept of PSDD grew out of my work on the impact of media and commercial culture on children. Children with PSDD frequently say they are bored. They have trouble becoming deeply engaged in unstructured activities. They do better when they are told what to do. They prefer structured activities at school, or DVDs to watch or videogames to play at home. They ask for new things all the time, but quickly become bored once they have them.

By their very nature, children's relationships with each other require endless problem solving: for instance, to work out how to respond appropriately to the behaviour of the other, how to co-ordinate behaviours in order to work together co-operatively, and what to do when a conflict arises to resolve it peacefully. PSDD undermines children's ability to develop these problem-solving skills.

So sexy so soon?

The marketing to girls of sexualized appearance also influences their behaviour and relationships. Recently, I was in Belfast, leading a workshop for early childhood educators on the sexualization of early childhood. When the highly popular Bratz dolls came up, the room filled with groans. "Why the groans?" I asked. They were worried about the focus on appearance and sexiness that the "Bratz culture" encouraged. They saw young girls using the dolls primarily for one thing—to dress them up for fashion shows, and then to imitate, themselves, those fantasized behaviours they had their dolls perform.

The "Bratz" ideal also becomes a model for their self-identity. In the USA, a mother told me she overheard her seven-year-old daughter, Jenna, talking with friends about what they could do to get their mothers to buy them shirts to expose their belly buttons. They wanted to be like "April, the popular girl in their class, the girl whom the boys reallllllllly like". One child said she would get her grandma to buy it for her since her mother would not. Another said she had been asking and asking and thought that, finally, her mother would get it for her for her birthday. Then one girl started talking about how mean her mother was because "she would never buy her a belly button shirt; her mother really didn't care if no one liked her at school". The others agreed this was a "really mean mother".

Then there is Sandra, the mother of a girl who had recently entered middle school, who told me this story. "Last week I took my daughter Alyssa shopping for a dress for her first middle school dance. We started out with such happy anticipation. But I couldn't believe the dresses I had to veto because of the length (almost up to her crotch) or the neckline (a lot of cleavage), the completely missing backs, or the clinginess—or sometimes all of the above. We both got more and more tense. Finally, Alyssa burst into tears and lashed out at me, 'You're so mean! Drew and Bryn chose their own dresses! I just won't go to the dance. Forget it.' She stormed out of the store. I felt like I was caught in a vice. I wasn't going to let her out of the house looking like a hooker. But I hated how setting this limit wrought such havoc on our relationship. And to be honest, there really weren't many appealing choices of more conservative dresses."

Each of these stories captures how the commercial culture is using sexiness to teach young girls to judge themselves and others based on how they look, what they can buy, and what they wear. When they dress up their Bratz doll in the new outfit and prance her around, or get the new belly button shirt or sexy dance dress, their happiness seems assured. But their pleasure is fleeting as they soon seek the next fad item in order to look right and feel good.

In these stories, too, we see that the girls have developed "needs" that are inappropriate to their current age. Also, they are struggling to deal with information they are too young to understand fully or put into a meaningful context. This is what the marketing industry often calls *age compression*—getting children involved in issues at increasingly younger ages. What better way to ensure that society produces a generation of hungry consumers, who are always looking for the next thing to make them popular?

Under these circumstances, it has become difficult for children to develop and sustain the capacity for caring, as they relate better to things than to people. Instead, they are learning that it is how you look, not what you do, which defines how people feel about and treat each other. They are learning to conform to a very narrow range of acceptable appearances and behaviours. Moreover, they are acting out *premature adolescent rebellions* as they come to see their parents, to whom they should still be turning for guidance and support in the early years, as the enemy! Is it any wonder that Public Agenda (2002) surveyed parents and found that over three-quarters of them said they thought it is harder raising children today than it was for their parents? In addition, almost half of the parents surveyed said their biggest worry was "raising a child who is well behaved and has good values".

Increases in aggression and bullying?

A concerned parent wrote asking for advice about the following situation:

> I bought my 6-year-old son, Derrick, Lego "Alpha Team" toys. You follow the directions to make various characters that are designated as "good" or "bad" guy figures. Now the Alpha Team figures have led to trouble on the playground for Derrick and his friends. As they act out the "good guy" characters, they choose an unsuspecting kid on the playground to be the "bad guy". Then they (the "good guys") attack the "bad guy" who ends up in tears. My son and his friends wind up at the principal's office for bullying, where they keep trying to explain that they are just "pretending". This has happened three times in the past month, and now the parents of the boys involved have been called in for a conference. [Levin & Carlsson-Paige, 2007, pp. 11–12]

In October of 2006, an elementary school in Massachusetts banned "tag" during recess because children (primarily boys) were hurting each other when they played the game. School administrators were worried that the injuries children were receiving during the game could lead to legal action from parents, and, therefore, felt they had no choice but to impose the ban (Cromley, 2006). This was not the first school in the USA that has placed such limits on this game. There have been numerous news reports of traditional games like tag and dodge ball games, long loved by children, being banned in other schools (for instance, see Bazar, 2006).

In my first example here, we see boys caught up in a view of the world as divided between the "good" and the "bad", and, because "good guys are 'good' ", they can do whatever they think will work to get the "bad guy sorted". They are confused about fantasy and reality and are not thinking in advance about the effects of their actions on the child who has been labelled as "the bad guy". In short, they are doing real world things that they learned from the pretend world, and it is having real world effects. The Lego toy described above is but one example of the hundreds of structured toys being marketed to children, often through the violent media, that focus boys' attention and play on doing combat; where are the positive lessons about how best to treat others and develop caring relationships? In the second example, we see how the anti-social behaviours that the boys have learnt can transfer into everyday play and threaten the quality of playground relationships (Levin & Carlsson-Paige, 2006).

In both examples, children are hurting each other and seem to have little regard for the effects of their actions on their victims. Is it any wonder that the instances of childhood bullying and anti-social behaviour are now rising? While our consumer culture is certainly not the sole cause of violent behaviour in children (a child's early attachment experiences figure significantly in their predisposition to violence and their methods of problem solving), we cannot underestimate the power of the media and the marketing of violent images to diminish children's capacity to develop co-operative and compassionate ways of relating.

Compassion deficit disorder

The ability to relate to, empathize with, and have compassion for others builds slowly out of what children experience in their early attachments and from their wider relational and cultural environments. Through social interaction, children learn the valuable skills of connecting effectively to get their needs met and to value the needs of others. However, the more we give children objects that remove them from relationships and that limit their experience of "self empowerment" (rather than *power over* others), the more they miss out on the gradual construction of those skills that mutual and positive relationships require.

In this chapter, we have presented numerous examples of children who seem disengaged from the kinds of activities that promote co-operation and compassion. Assailed by the sounds of whistles on cribs, stimulated by the market to desire things to make them feel good, and encouraged by television programmes to do battle against the "bad guys", children now have fewer opportunities to build upon the comfort and security that loving interactions with parents should give, and to establish caring and mutual connections with friends. Children absorb messages from the media about what is desirable in themselves and in relationships with others. Our popular culture frames systems of social expectations that work against the development of the capacity to form healthy connections.

Even securely attached children may struggle to navigate their way through the complex messages of consumer culture, but, at least, these children are likely to have a vital internal relational model through which to engage with others. However, insecurely attached children, already struggling with an uneasy sense of self, might find the messages harder to accommodate and may invest in consumer objects and combative modes of relating in order to gain a sense of safety that is both compelling and fragile. The pop cultural risks to relational life are compounded by the pressure on parents to meet their children's needs—needs that are too often manufactured by commerce and, by their nature, difficult to satisfy.

In sum, we are raising a generation of children who are at risk of developing, metaphorically speaking, "compassion deficit disorder" (CDD)—the inability to empathize with others or to relate to others with mutual care and affection!

What we can do

Aggressive commercial culture makes the process of parenting and enabling secure attachments with children difficult. It shapes the ways that parents understand "what children need" for their emotional development, and their judgements about how best those needs can be met. It also undermines parents' ability to resist, comfortably, children's consuming desires for objects in which they invest their sense of worth. Yet, failure to resist might well bring the parent and child into conflict, undermining a child's sense of security and increasing their risk of developing CDD. Herein lies the challenge: how can we *limit* the harm that is being done by commercial culture and build secure attachments with children? Unfortunately, many of today's most common responses to disturbed social behaviour by children fail miserably at meeting this challenge.

Blaming the victim or just saying "No"?

Often, when children behave in ways that hurt or upset others, adults respond by blaming the children and punishing them for what they did. This response assumes that the children both understand what they are doing and choose to do it. By punishing or shaming them, the thinking goes, children will behave with compassion the next time. However, in sending them to the principal's office, or banning their playground games, we are shifting the responsibility for their actions away from the media and other cultural pressures and placing it on their young shoulders. I would argue that if children do not know how to play without causing harm, it is the job of adults to help them to play more safely. That is how we can counter the messages that commercial cultures are conveying.

Similarly, we need to get beyond the *just say no* approach. By trying to "say no" to Bratz dolls, belly-button shirts, sexy party dresses, and ignoring children's interests and concerns, we are distancing ourselves from what is important to them. We are removing ourselves from opportunities to guide our children and influence them in meaningful ways.

Working together

Once we recognize the power of popular culture in shaping our children and our parenting, there are several things we can do to help children navigate the messages of commercial culture while maintaining healthy adult–children communication and enabling the development of children's interpersonal skills and understanding. Fundamentally, the process requires that we work *with* children in ways that help them build a secure sense of self.

- We can work to limit exposure to the high tech, media and commercial cultures as much as possible when children are

young. The longer we can delay this exposure, the more opportunities children have to build a healthy sense of self, and a
repertoire of skills for relating with others.
- We can help children make sense of the things to which they are
  exposed. One of the best ways to do this is to stay connected
  with children around these issues. For instance, we can have
  conversations with children that allow us to discover and value
  what they know and think, and then base our responses on
  what children say (for examples of this kind of conversation,
  see Levin & Kilbourne, in press).
- We can try to influence the lessons that children are learning
  about relationships and how to participate in them. Too often,
  schools are sacrificing opportunities for children to develop
  social knowledge and skills in favour of intensified academic
  instruction. The social curriculum is now so important, and
  there are many resources to help with this.
- We can work with other adults in children's lives, such as other
  family members, other parents and teachers, to support each
  other's efforts to promote children's positive social development and relationships.
- We can work within our communities, with organizations and
  with policymakers to try to change, in big and little ways, the
  current economic environment that has made the commercial
  and media cultures such a powerful force in children's lives.

> We can try to influence the lessons that children are learning
> about relationships and how to participate in them. Too often,
> schools are sacrificing opportunities for children to develop social
> knowledge and skills in favor of intensified academic instruction.
> The social curriculum is now so important, and there are many
> resources to help with this. [Levin, 2003]

References

Bazar, E. (2006). Not it! More schools ban games at recess. *USA Today*,
    26 June. www.usatoday.com/news/health/2006–06–26-recess-
    bans_x.htm (accessed 26 May 2007).
Bowlby, J. (1969). *Attachment and Loss. Vol. 1: Attachment* (2nd edn).
    New York: Basic Books, 1982.

Cromley, J. (2006). Tag, you're out! *Los Angeles Times*, 6 November. www.latimes.com/news/education/la-he-tag6nov06,1,4374880. story?coll=la-news-learning (accessed 6 November 2006).

Levin, D. (1998). *Remote Control Childhood? Combating the Hazards of Media Culture*. Washington, DC: National Association for the Education of Young Children.

Levin, D. (2003). *Teaching Young Children in Violent Times: Building a Peaceable Classroom* (2nd edn). Cambridge, MA: Educators for Social Responsibility and Washington, DC: National Association for the Education of Young Children.

Levin, D. (2007). Problem solving deficit disorder: creative versus programmed play in Korea and the United States. In: E. Goodenough (Ed.), *Where Do the Children Play? A Study Guide*. Detroit, MI: Wayne University Press.

Levin, D., & Carlsson-Paige, N. (2007). *The War Play Dilemma: What Every Parent and Teacher Needs to Know* (2nd edn). New York: Teachers College Press.

Levin, D., & Kilbourne, J. (2008). *So Sexy So Soon: The Sexualization of Childhood and What Parents Can Do to Protect Their Kids*.. New York: Ballantine.

Levin, D., & Rosenquest, B. (2001). The increasing role of electronic toys in the lives of infants and toddlers: should we be concerned? *Contemporary Issues in Early Childhood*, 2(2): 242–247.

Linn, S. (2005). *Consuming Kids: Protecting Our Children from the Onslaught of Marketing and Advertising*. New York: Anchor.

Meltz, B. (2004). There are benefits to boredom. *Boston Globe*, 22 January. www.boston.com/yourlife/family/articles/2004/01/22/there_are_benefits_to_boredom (accessed 27 May 2007).

Public Agenda (2002). *"Easier Said Than Done" Parents Talk about Raising Children in Today's America: A Report from Public Agenda*. www.publicagenda.org/research/research_reports_details.cfm?list=15. Accessed 23 October 2003.

Rideout, V., Vandewater, E., & Wartella, E. (2003). *Zero to Six: Electronic Media in the Lives of Infants, Toddlers and Preschoolers*. Menlo Park, CA: Kaiser Family Foundation.

Roberts, D., Foehr, U., & Rideout, V. (2005). *Generation M: Media in the Lives of 8–18 Year Olds*. Menlo Park, CA: Kaiser Family Foundation.

Schor, J. (2005). *Born to Buy: The Commercialized Child and the New Consumer Culture*. New York: Scribner.

White, R. (1959). Motivation reconsidered: the concept of competence. *Psychological Review*, 66: 297–333.

CHAPTER SEVEN

Primitive justice: who pays the price?[1]

Jack A. Cole

I n 1970 a terrible policy was adopted by the USA, one that would prove to have a dramatic impact on social and familial attachment. It was called the "War on Drugs". The drug war implemented old laws that had been generally ignored for fifty-six years, and also created new, harsher laws, which set mandatory minimum incarceration sentences for violators, sentences that are completely counterproductive. These laws prohibit the production, distribution, and use of certain drugs by anyone. There is little rhyme or reason for the drugs that were picked for prohibition, since none of them seems as dangerous to individuals or society as tobacco and alcohol. In the USA, 430,000 people die each year as a result of ingesting tobacco; another 85,000 die from ingesting alcohol. Only 12,000 people die each year from ingesting all the illegal drugs combined, including heroin, cocaine, methamphetamine, Phencyclidine, LSD, and Ecstasy (Bennett, 2008, p. 2). Furthermore, there has not been a single recorded death in history from the ingestion of cannabis (Mokdad, Marks, Stroup, & Gerberdine, 2004).

The US "War on Drugs" has destroyed relationships more consistently than any policy short of war against another country. Indeed, it has waged an internal and eternal war against our own people—our children, our parents, and ourselves. During the thirty-seven years this terrible war has been raging, the USA has spent more than one trillion tax dollars on its prosecution, made nearly thirty-eight million arrests for non-violent drug offences, and imprisoned millions for those violations.

During my twenty-six-year career in the New Jersey State Police—fourteen years as an undercover narcotics officer—I witnessed the terrible unintended consequences of this failed policy.

Who gets arrested? Who goes to jail?

The United States is a very punitive society. We imprison our population at a rate seven times that of the most punitive Western European countries, who incarcerate at rates between sixty-seven and 148 per hundred thousand (Currie, 1998, p. 15). The USA imprisons 1009 per hundred thousand (Pew Center, 2008). This figure represents the world's largest per capita rate of incarceration. It is a constantly expanding figure because of the uniquely catastrophic way drug prohibition fuels the prison-industrial complex of the USA. Figure 1 dramatically illustrates the drug war's contribution to our skyrocketing imprisonment figures. At the beginning of the "war" in 1970, prisoners in federal facilities for non-violent drug offences numbered 3384, while 17,302 were there for all other offences, including crimes of violence. By the year 2005, while we had increased incarcerations for crimes of violence by 294%, we had swelled the ranks of those in prison for non-violent drug offences by 2,558% (FBI, 2005, pp. 278–280).

Within these shocking statistics lay another reality: to find a more virulent racism than that employed by the drug laws one would have to look back to slavery in the USA. The American white upper-class seldom has to fear arrest and prosecution for drug violations, but the black community has been devastated by arrest and imprisonment. Despite the fact that drug laws apply to everyone, the implementation of those laws is accomplished in a manner revealed by statistics as blatantly racist.

According to the 1998 Federal Housing Survey, 72% of drug users and dealers are white, while only 14% are black. Yet 37% of all people arrested for drug violations in the USA are black; 81% of

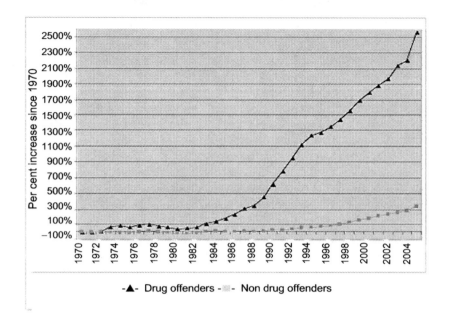

Figure 1.   Increase of prisoners in US Federal Custody from 1970 to 2005.
Source: US Bureau of Statistics.

all drug violators in federal prison are black, and 60% of all drug violators in state prisons are black (SAMHSA, 1998, p. 13). By 2004, we were imprisoning whites at the rate of 717, and blacks at the rate of 4,919, per hundred thousand (Harrison & Beck, 2005, pp. 2, 11). Even the Apartheid government of South Africa imprisoned blacks in 1993 only at the rate of 851 per hundred thousand (Mauer, 1994, p. 1)—a large number, but nowhere near as large as 4,919.

Four years ago I read one of the saddest statements imaginable in the FBI's Uniform Crime Report: a young couple giving birth to a black male baby has an expectation of one in three that their child will serve time in prison. What must a young couple think when the mother gives birth to a black male baby? How much hope can black couples have for their child's future when faced with the enormity of the drug war's impact on family life? If we changed only one word in the FBI's sentence—"black" male baby to "white" male baby—we would have ended the war on drugs thirty years ago because the people in power would never have accepted that terrible outcome applied to whites.

Equally dramatic has been the impact of black incarceration rates on American democracy. Many state laws decree that no one convicted of a felony can vote. Nearly all drug violations are felonies, and because we arrest seven times as many black men per capita for drug felonies as white men, fourteen per cent of all black male US voters have lost their right to vote. In Texas and Florida, states both governed by the Bush dynasty, 31% of black men have been disenfranchized (Beck & Mumola, 1999, p. 10).

There are more black men in US prisons today than there were male slaves in 1840 (US Census Bureau, 2007) and they are used for the same purpose—to make a great deal of money for those in power. They work at sixteen to twenty cents per hour for corporations under the conscript labour system. Prisons in the USA are being privatized, and those who head them have hired lobbyists to pressure Congress to create laws that would impose longer mandatory minimum sentences for drug violations. It is almost unnecessary to add that they do this to guarantee an ever-expanding captive population from which they can profit. In a twenty-year period, the number of US prisons has quadrupled, making prison-building our fastest-growing industry. Prisons for profit do not belong in a democratic society.

The USA's war on drugs has not achieved a single stated goal. Instead, its direct result has been continuously to escalate rates of death, disease, crime, and addiction. Human relationships are destroyed, which causes the problem to be self-perpetuating and constantly expanding. According to the Federal Drug Enforcement Administration, before this war started in 1970 there were four million people in the USA who had used illegal drugs. Thirty years later, there were 110 million people who had used illegal drugs. The impact on social cohesion and familial attachment includes high levels of domestic and community violence, homicide, and ever-greater substance abuse.

What is the effect of the arrest of a young adult parent? If not destroyed, his or her life is certainly crippled, and so is that of his or her family. A conviction will hound this person every day for the rest of his or her life. Every time they seek a job, the conviction hangs over their head like an ugly cloud. Employers look at their record and say, "Druggie, we don't want you!" Indeed, no one wants them. The only place that welcomes them is the very drug culture from which drug-war policy claims to save them.

This policy has become a numbers game, spreading a vast net that ensnares the guilty and the innocent alike. Through drug testing in schools and workplaces, drug warriors search out drug users before a crime is even committed. If a young person fails a drug test, he or she is expelled from school or loses employment. When caught with even one cannabis cigarette, in most states the person loses his or her driver's licence. In rural or suburban America, where there is no public transportation, this person can no longer get to school or be gainfully employed. If they reside in urban centres that have public transportation but happen to live in government subsidized housing, we will not only throw them out of the house but their whole family will also be evicted, and, if they live with their grandparents, those old folks will also have to hit the street, because the US Supreme Court ruled in November 2003 that this kind of massive punishment is OK. It is OK because, according to them, "We are fighting a war on drugs," and when you fight a war, nearly anything is acceptable (Department of Housing and Urban Development v. Rucker et al., 2002).

As if this were not enough, we also tell the individual he or she can no longer get a government grant or loan to go to college. (The Federal law that imposes this draconian punishment is the 1998 Higher Education Act.) But, in the crazy paradox of the drug war, if the same person had been convicted of rape or murder he or she could get the loan.

The result for a young person is a downward spiral from which recovery is very difficult, if not impossible. Loss of job and educational possibilities is incapacitating. It makes people unable to provide for themselves or their families. A resulting sense of worthlessness and despair damages their friendships and family relationships. Parents, children, and spouses find it difficult to deal with the offenders. This alienation of family removes the individual's hope for a better future and simultaneously any reason why he or she might stop using drugs. The last stop in this terrible voyage is prison. There are more than 2.3 million people in US prisons today (Harrison & Beck, 2005, p. 1), a per capita rate far larger than that of any other country in the world. To put this number in context, right here in what we like to call "the land of freedom" we have 4.6% of the world's population (US Census Bureau, 2003) but 22.5% of its prisoners (Walmsley, 2003, p. 1). The majority of these prisoners have been jailed for non-violent drug offences. For instance, over the thirty-seven years of the drug war, while the rate of Federal imprisonment has increased by 294% for violent crimes, it has increased by 2,558% for non-violent drug offences (FBI, 2005).

Jailing always brings family dislocation but in the USA it often entails vast geographical dislocation. The USA invests sixty-nine billion dollars every year to make another 1.9 million arrests for non-violent drug offences. State governments are hard pressed to supply enough money to imprison all of the convicted individuals at the average annual rate of $25,000 per person (Paige & Beck, 2006, p. 9). So, states with high costs of living export their prisoners to states with low ones. Thus, a young person who is convicted in Massachusetts may end up serving his or her sentence in Texas, 2000 miles away from relatives. Or a person convicted in Hawaii may serve their sentence in California, to where families cannot even drive, but must purchase airline tickets for visits—hopeless for any but the well-to-do. Thus, it becomes practically impossible for families to visit such displaced offenders or continue any face-to-face relationship.

To make things worse, corporate America capitalizes on these prisoners. Telephone companies vie for contracts with prisons because prisoners can make only collect calls home. The company winning the contract charges between six and ten times as much for a collect call from a prison as it does for a collect call from anywhere else. Then it kicks back some of its profit to the prison to guarantee the contract. Hence, these prisoners cannot even continue their fractured relationships by phone because calling is simply too expensive.

Once the offender has been released, myriad problems surge up. Lone parents must balance child-care with finding and retaining a job—always difficult under any circumstance but, for the reasons we have already described, far more difficult for the drug offender. Once the parent has found employment, he or she must find good child-care—a scarce resource in America for any but the financially secure. Families affected by the drug war are far more likely than other families to have their children removed by the state. For example, a woman who uses crack cocaine or methamphetamine while pregnant is liable to lose her baby to forced foster care. In North Carolina, hospitals have reported to prosecutors the results of blood tests of pregnant mothers so that this law could be enforced. While there are many good foster parents, the quality of foster care in America is not good overall. And it is certain that an explosion of children into the system via the drug war creates unbearable strains.

I know that if I spent ten years trying to devise the policy best guaranteed to create the next generation of children addicted to hard drugs, I could not come up with a better policy than the war on drugs, which makes orphans of children by imprisoning their parents. I would bet that the single best predictor of substance abuse and premature death among adolescents is the incarceration of a parent on drug charges.

I cannot emphasize enough that the acts deemed criminal by the war on drugs have been designated as such only because someone decided they should be. The law defines two types of crime. *Malum in se* crimes comprise acts such as murder, rape, robbery, and arson, which violate the nature, morals, and public principles of a civilized society. *Malum prohibitum* crimes exist because, at a given time, a particular government decides that they should exist. Certain of these are often referred to as consensual crimes. Examples include violations of drug laws, prostitution, homosexuality, and "miscegenation". Ingesting a drug, which means putting in your body something another person does not want to put in his or her body, is today a consensual crime. In other words, it is an activity that should not be a crime at all. Depending on the date and the country involved, the drug of choice in a drug crime could be alcohol, tobacco, sugar, or even coffee, all prohibited at various points in history and later allowed. For instance, in the 1500s, in the region now comprising the Baltic nations, possession of coffee was a capital offence that carried a sentence of decapitation.

Not only is there abundant evidence that the USA's policy on drugs directly disrupts attachments and a child's sense of security, it is also clear that government supporters of the policy actively resist campaigns to alleviate the disruption to family life and the generational effects created by the policy. I am the executive director of an international non-profit educational organization called Law Enforcement Against Prohibition (www.LEAP.cc). It was created to give voice to law enforcers around the world who believe, as we do, that the USA's policy of drug prohibition is not only a failure, but that it is a self-perpetuating, ever-expanding policy disaster. LEAP's 10,000 members know it is far more efficient and ethical to legalize and regulate all drugs and to treat drug-abuse as a health problem, not as a crime.

Resistance to drug-law reform is fuelled, first and foremost, by the profits generated by the war on drugs. During its thirty-seven-year history, the war on drugs has produced more than a trillion tax dollars for law-enforcement agencies. Billions more are generated annually from sales of property seized as a result of the USA's forfeiture laws, laws that quite literally give the government a licence to steal (Levy, 1996). Forfeiture laws are the only US statutes under which an accused is guilty until found innocent. In Austin v. United States, the US Court of Appeals for the Eighth Circuit wrote:

> We are troubled by the government's view that any property, whether it be a hobo's hovel or the Empire State Building, can be seized by the government because the owner, regardless of his or her past criminal record, engages in a single drug transaction. (Austin v. United States, 1992, p. 818).

Twenty per cent of all police budgets in my country can be traced directly to the war on drugs and the vast fortunes amassed as a result of these forfeiture laws, which are used to help fund municipal and state budgets (Stossel, 2002). And an obvious consequence of the profit motive is the explosion of the USA's private prison service, now the country's fourth largest and fastest growing industry.

And, of course, hand-in-hand with the profit motive that fuels resistance to drug-policy reform goes racism. As shown above, the criminal justice system targets the Black and Latino poor, who are greatly over-represented in the prison system.

What can be done?

The prestige of government has undoubtedly been lowered considerably by the Prohibition law. For nothing is more destructive of respect for the government and the law of the land than passing laws which cannot be enforced. It is an open secret that the danger-ous increase of crime in this country is closely connected with this. [Einstein, 1921]

The great myth of the drug war is that drug use causes a high inci-dence of death, disease, crime, and addiction. But, in fact, it is drug prohibition itself that creates most of these social ills. The only solu-tion is ending prohibition, just as the alcohol prohibition so accu-rately described by Einstein in 1921 was finally ended in 1933. There is little difference between alcohol prohibition and drug prohibition. What difference does exist made the situation better under alcohol prohibition. For instance, under alcohol prohibition only sellers and distributors were arrested, not users. The Reagan administration initiated the drive to incarcerate users. And so we now enforce a policy that mandates arresting our children in order to save them.

Just as alcohol became a regulated substance whose production and sale has adhered ever since to government-established norms, so "hard" as well as "soft" drugs must be legalized and then placed under strict regulation. For many Americans, the notion of across-the-board drug legalization conjures up nightmares of mass addic-tion. But our history proves the opposite. For the first 138 years of our history—1776 to 1914—all drugs were legal in the United States. For example, advertisements for heroin as a cough suppres-sor indicated that anyone could buy an ounce of heroin off grocery store shelves for a mere $4.85 (Figure 2). Today, thanks to the war on drugs, an ounce of pure heroin is worth between $8,505 and $77,678, depending on whether you are buying it in San Diego, California or St Louis, Missouri (DEA, 2005). Codeine was accepted, matter of factly, as an over-the-counter drug. But in 1914 the government estimated the rate of drug addiction in the USA at 1.3%, so they passed the Harrison Anti-Drug Act, effectively mak-ing heroin illegal (Kane, 2004, p. 45). Today, after nearly a hundred years of illegal drug laws and thirty-seven years of prosecuting a war on drugs, 1.3% of the population of the USA is addicted to drugs (Robinson & Scherlen, 2007, p. 94).

Examples from other countries demonstrate that legalization does not result in increased drug use. In the Netherlands, drugs have

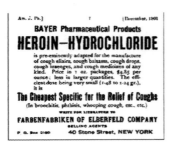

Figure 2.   A 1901 advertisement for over-the-counter heroin.

been virtually legal since 1976. The police there simply look the other way unless user or seller is fighting or causing some other kind of trouble. Using cannabis and hashish in Amsterdam is exactly like using alcohol in the USA. If you are an adult, you casually enter a "brown bar" and order from a menu that offers a multiple choice between various brands of either drug. You may smoke your five grams wherever you wish—in the bar, on the street, or at home.

The result is that in the Netherlands, cannabis and hashish use are as mundane as alcohol use in our country. The drugs' acceptance among legislators and law-enforcers has influenced their use among the Netherlands' youth, and the difference between them and our own adolescents is striking. A USA survey has shown that while 28% of Dutch tenth-graders had tried cannabis, 41% of their American counterparts had used the drug (Van Bakel, 2002, p. 128). Moreover, Netherlands per capita use, by people of all ages, of soft drugs, cannabis and hashish, is half what it is in the USA (Abraham, Cohen, Van Til, & de Winter, 1999, pp. 39–45).

There is no "drug czar" in the Netherlands. Drug abuse is treated not as a crime there, but as an illness, so responsibility for overseeing drugs policy rests with the Netherlands' Minister of Health. When American researchers interviewed him to learn why the startling thirteen per cent discrepancy existed between Netherlands and American early-teens, he observed, "We have managed to make pot boring." Dutch children know that when they turn eighteen, they can go to the neighbourhood "brown bar" and get all the cannabis they want. While their American peers begin using drugs at the "entry-level age" of fourteen, Dutch youth wait out the formative four years from fourteen to eighteen to decide whether or not to use drugs at all. Netherlands drug policy distinguishes soft- from hard-drug purchases. Soft drugs are readily and legally available in coffee shops. Thus, users are not forced to buy their cannabis from the sorts of criminal dealers who, in the USA, use cannabis and hashish street sales to promote hard drugs like heroin, cocaine, and methamphetamine. The result is dramatic: in the USA the per capita use of hard drugs is four times that of the Netherlands. Moreover, the Netherlands' homicide rate is only one-fourth the per capita rate of the United States. Finally, drug-related law enforcement is far cheaper in the Netherlands at one-sixth the per capita money spent enforcing the USA's drug-war laws.

Comparative drug and violence indicators in the USA and the Netherlands

Table 1 summarizes the prevalence of drug use in the USA compared with that in the Netherlands.

Hand in hand with legalization should go regulation—strict controls for quality, potency, and standardized measurement in drugs produced in the USA or imported from other countries. The comparison, once again, is with the termination of alcohol prohibition. When alcohol was illegal, it became a fertile terrain for crime and unregulated production. Clandestine stills proliferated all sorts of adulterated "bathtub gins" and other harmful brews, with a resulting high incidence of death, injury, and disease.

Controlling and regulating drugs would virtually end drug overdoses. These deaths are a result of drug prohibition, not drug pharmacology. Just as "bathtub gin" produced deaths and internal physical damage, so adulterated heroin, for instance, or wildly vacillating pure-drug-to-cutting-agent ratios produce America's drug overdoses. An individual ingesting one street dealer's product that has a low heroin-to-cutting-agent ratio may suffer no harm, but

Table 1. Comparison of soft and hard drug use between young people in the USA and in the Netherlands.

Social indicator	Year	USA	Netherlands
Lifetime prevalence of cannabis use (ages 12+)	2001	37%	17%
Past month prevalence of cannabis use (ages 12+)	2001	5.4%	3.0%
Lifetime prevalence of heroin use (ages 12+)	2001	1.4%	0.4%
Incarceration rate per 100,000 population	2002	704	100
Per capita spending on drug-related law enforcement	1998	$379	$223
Homicide rate per 100,000 population	1999–2001 average	5.56	1.52

Source: Drug War Facts, Victoria, BC, Canada: Common Sense for Drug Policy, 2004, p. 144.

another individual ingesting a "hot shot"—heroin with little cutting agent added —will die. The user simply does not know what he or she is getting when buying a seller's unregulated product. Standardization would end this terrible game of Russian roulette.

Those saved from overdose death are at least available for our attempts at weaning them off their addiction. If we, like our Dutch counterparts, view addiction as a health problem, our view of drugs and drug users changes. Both are no longer demonized. With this change in perspective comes at least the partial restoration of our own human relationships to the users who are often our children, parents, sisters, and brothers. Drug law reform should aim at bringing them back into our society as productive citizens. By contrast, the drug war buries these people before they have died, warehousing them in prisons and, afterwards, shoving them back into drug-culture oblivion.

Free distribution of maintenance doses

When addicted people wake up in the morning their only thought is where to get their "fix". If they know a seller, their next thought is, "How do I pay for it?" If they have the money, then they worry about whether the dealer will cheat them by selling them talcum powder, or kill them by selling them a "hot shot", or just beat and rob them.

A legalization and regulation programme would eliminate the constant worry and chaos of the user's life by instituting free maintenance dose distribution. It would normalize the user's relationships with friends and family by removing the stigma imposed by criminal sanctions. Switzerland and the Netherlands have both instituted projects that treat users by giving them government heroin—the closest thing in the world to legalized regulation of all drugs. If you can legalize and regulate heroin, you can legalize and regulate all drugs. This reform has produced a decline in the incidence of drug use. Across both countries health clinics have been established. Drug addicts are allowed to inject government heroin up to three times a day in these clinics, using clean needles, under medical supervision. According to British Columbia Medical Health Officer Perry Kendall,

> Heroin, if it's used on a maintenance basis, in pharmacological doses without any risk of overdose or contamination, is actually a very safe drug. It doesn't harm the liver, doesn't harm the kidneys per se, and it doesn't kill brain cells . . . [CATV News Service, 2006]

The staff of these clinics provide a vital link to social stability— social workers, educators, and job specialists who work to wean their clients off heroin. Because they see the addicts three times a day, they become trusted friends. Friends are certainly more influential in encouraging behaviour change than a judge who orders "rehabilitation" and then only sees the addict again after receiving a report of a failed drug test, to remand him or her to prison.

Dramatic statistics show the outcomes of these policies. In Switzerland, thanks to a quality controlled drug production programme initiated in 1994, there has not been an overdose death. Because drug users in Switzerland now use clean needles, Switzerland now has the lowest per capita rate of AIDS and hepatitis of any country in Europe.

According to Nordt and Stohler (2006) moreover, the Swiss programme has had a dramatic impact on other social ills, of the kind that plague the USA in the drug war. Cocaine use among heroin addicts has plummeted from 35% to 5%. Crime has been slashed by 60%. Users do not have to prostitute themselves, nor do they need to steal to pay for their drugs. There are no heroin dealers on the streets; the drugs are free (*ibid.*). Thus, there are no shooting wars in drug turf competitions. (When was the last time you heard of two beer distributors shooting it out over who was going to supply the local tavern? One might reach for his pocket, and instead of pulling out a gun pull out a piece of paper, declaring, "I have a contract for this territory. I'll take you to court.")

In Switzerland no police are killed while fighting a useless war. No innocent adults are killed while many die tragically in the USA because police mistake them for armed drug felons (Balko, 2006, pp. 1–98).

In the Netherlands, no children are killed in crossfire, while in the USA during 2002, in Detroit alone, eleven children were shot by drug dealers trying to protect their turf (Hackney & Schmitt, 2002, p. 1).

And in Switzerland, with no drug dealers in the streets, young novices are not enticed to start using heroin. Indeed, according to a June 2006 report about the Swiss project in the prestigious medical journal, *Lancet*, over the past ten years Zurich has "seen an 82 per cent decline in new users of heroin" (Nordt & Stohler, 2006, p. 1833). Every other country except the Netherlands has realized more new heroin users than they predicted ten years ago. Legalized regulation of drugs really works.

When you consider the web of human relationships that comprise the Swiss programme—medical staff, social workers, and other counsellors—one in which addicts gain new friends and advisers who stay with them for the long haul, these statistics are not surprising. Secure and sustained human connection, in the end, is at the core of solving or perpetuating the problem of drug abuse and addiction. Destroy those connections and attachments and you get outcomes such as we experienced in the USA. Once a society begins to view the addict as ill and in need of help, as disconnected from relationships and in need of support, it can build programmes that work; programmes that not only treat drug abuse medically, that not only remove the profit motive for drug distribution and hence the crime and corruption, but that give the drug dependent and the addicted the vision of a new future, and hence hope for a better life.

The USA is the richest country in the world, but every year it determines it must spend sixty-nine billion dollars to destroy lives rather than help people put them back together—to alienate rather then ameliorate. If we were to take a portion of those sixty-nine billion dollars saved annually thanks to ending drug prohibition, we could redirect it in two ways. First, we could create programmes similar to those offered in Switzerland—ones that offer hope. In the more than thirty-five years during which I have worked in this field I have found that addicted people have one thing in common—little or no hope for the future. Give them hope and they can leave drugs behind them.

United States' history bears out my point. Many soldiers used marijuana during the early part of the Vietnam War (Ingraham, 1967, p. 10) because they had been placed in an untenable position—one in which hope was virtually non-existent. When President Nixon learned of the prevalence of marijuana among the troop, he initiated an enforcement programme that tracked the users down and forced them to quit. The programme was quite successful because the odour of marijuana was so easy to detect. But the policy had terrible unintended side effects—most of the American troops simply switched to the cheaper, more easily concealed #4 grade heroin, available all over the country (Baum, 1996, pp. 52–55; McCoy, 1991, p. 240). This was super-potent and could be smoked with tobacco or ingested by chewing toothpicks that had been dipped in a liquid heroin solution. Countless soldiers were thus exposed to regular heroin use over a long period. At the end of their tours the soldiers were ordered to stay until they could produce clean urine samples. Given that powerful incentive—coercive, but one that carried the hope of seeing family and friends once again—they all cleaned up and returned home (Lifton, 1973; Siegel, 1989, p. 305). Contrary to a US media myth, according to which the soldiers continued their addictions after discharge, a mere 5% ever returned to the drug once they were home. Their heroin abuse was prompted in Vietnam by hopelessness created by the loss of basic human relationships and fear of imminent death. I would maintain that the 5% that continued to use heroin after returning to the USA had no more hope for the future here than they did in Vietnam.

Hope is essential if we want to lower the incidence of drug addiction. Rehabilitation centres offering a way out of addictions might seem currently to offer such hope. But at present, two-thirds of hard drug-addicted people who come begging for help find there is no room at the inn. That is because of the "zero tolerance" attitude fostered by prohibition, and the resulting fact that judges give youngsters caught smoking a Friday night joint the choice between rehab and jail. Ordering rehabilitation for a pot-smoker is far less urgent or reasonable than ordering me to go to rehab because I will drink a Jack Daniels after I finish writing this tonight. And since courts are needlessly flooding rehabilitation centres with pot smokers, hard drug addicts must continue to go begging. We spend billions locking them up and have nothing left to help them end their addiction.

Hope can also rise on the wings of guaranteed minimums. Instead of creating more mandatory minimum sentences, what would happen if we spent some of the saved sixty-nine billion dollars to create mandatory minimum education for everyone; mandatory minimum health care; decent housing; jobs for everybody who wanted to work; mandatory livable—not just minimum—wages. And, to this list we must add mandatory regard for those attachments and affectional bonds that help sustain a sense of self, safety, and trust, and whose violations (not least by the War on Drugs) perpetuate suffering and social pathologies.

Another portion of those saved billions should fund real education about drugs. This does not mean the Drug Abuse Resistance Education (DARE), a notoriously failed programme that nevertheless is taught by police in the majority of schools in the USA (Shepard, 2002, pp. 1–11), but real programmes that tell the truth about drugs. That drug education works is borne out by our own history. By 1985, 42% of the adult US population smoked tobacco, the most deadly and addictive drug known to humankind. Smoking tobacco kills 430,000 people in the USA every year, while the use of all illicit drugs and the misuse of all prescription drugs combined kill fewer than 30,000 per year. We decided we had to do something about nicotine addiction but we did not start a war on tobacco and begin arresting users. We initiated a very strong drug education programme and by 2001 only 21% of the adult population of the USA smoked: the percentage is dropping every year (Center for Disease Control, 2007). What we at LEAP want to make clear to readers of this anthology is that the USA cut the use of the most addictive drug known to humankind in half and we did not have to send a single person to prison to make the campaign against smoking tobacco work; we did not have to destroy a single life. There are better ways of lowering the incidence of death, disease, crime, and addiction than prosecuting a failed war on drugs that continues to be nothing but disastrous for all our lives.

Note

1. This chapter was edited by Ellen Cantarow—many thanks.

References

Abraham, M. D., Cohen, P. D. A., van Til, R.-J., & de Winter, M. A. L. (1999). *Licit and Illicit Drug Use in the Netherlands, 1997*. University of Amsterdam, Centre for Drug Research, Amsterdam: University of Amsterdam, September; US Department of Health and Human Services, Substance Abuse and Mental Health Services Administration, *National Household Survey on Drug Abuse: Main Findings 1998*, Washington, DC: US Department of Health and Human Services, March 2000, pp. 18–24.

Austin v. United States, US Court of Appeals, Eighth Circuit (964 F. 2d 818 [1992]). www.answers.com/topic/austin-v-united-states.

Balko, R. (2006). *Overkill: The Rise of Paramilitary Police Raids in America*. Washington, DC: CATO Institute.

Baum, D. (1996). *Smoke and Mirrors: The War on Drugs and the Politics of Failure*. New York: Little, Brown.

Beck, A. J., & Mumola, C. J. (1999). *Prisoners in 1998*. Washington, DC: US Department of Justice, Bureau of Justice Statistics.

Bennett, W. C. (2008). www.briancbennett.com/charts/death/2004/intox-types.htm.

CATV (2006). Few joining study that offers free heroin. Canada Television News Service, 3 January. www.ctv.ca/servlet/ArticleNews/story/CTVNews/20060103/heroinstudy_20060103/20060103?hub=Health.

Center for Disease Control (2007). National Health Interview Surveys: 1965, 1970, 1974, 1978, 1980, 1983, 1985, 1987, 1990, 1993, 1995, 1997,

1999, 2001–2004. www.cdc.gov/tobacco/data_statistics/tables/ adult/table_2.htm. Last updated 28 February 2007.

Currie, E. (1998). *Crime and Punishment in America*. New York: Metropolitan Books, Henry Holt.

DEA, "Drug Intelligence Brief, 2002" (2005). *Domestic Monitoring Program Drug Intelligence Report*, US Drug Enforcement Administration, www.usdoj.gov/dea/pubs/intel/03057/03057.html#e, 24 July.

Department of Housing and Urban Development v. Rucker et al. (2002). Certiorari to the United States Court of Appeals for The Ninth Circuit, No. 00–1770. Argued February 19, 2002—Decided March 26, 2002. http://supreme.justia.com/us/535/125/case.html.

Drug War Facts (2004). Victoria, BC, Canada: *Common Sense for Drug Policy*. www.drugwarfacts.org/factbook.pdf

Einstein, A. (1982). *Ideas and Opinions* (based on *Mein Weltbild*, edited by Carl Seelig, and other sources), S. Bargmann (Trans.). New York: Crown.

Federal Bureau of Investigation (FBI) (2005). *Crime in the United States. Uniform Crime Reports 1981–2005*. Washington, DC: US Government Printing Office.

Hackney, S., & Schmitt, B. (2002). Homicide's tragic toll; 10 children dead in 16 weeks. *Detroit Free Press*, 14 May.

Harrison, P. M., & Beck, A. J. (2005). *Prison and Jail Inmates at Midyear 2004*. Bureau of Justice Statistics, Washington, DC: US Department of Justice, April.

Ingraham, L. (1967). US denies 75% of GIs in Vietnam use marijuana. *New York Times*, 28 December.

Kane, J. L. (2004). Policy is not a synonym for justice. In: B. Masters (Ed.), *The New Prohibition: Voices of Dissent Challenge the Drug War* (pp. 41–49). Lonedell, MO: Accurate Press.

Levy, L. W. (1996). *A License to Steal: The Forfeiture of Property*. London: The University of North Carolina Press.

Lifton, R. J. (1973). *Home From the War: Vietnam Veterans Neither Victims Nor Executioners*. New York: Simon & Schuster.

Mauer, M. (1994). *Americans Behind Bars: The International Use of Incarceration, 1992–1993*, The Sentencing Project, September. www.druglibrary.org/schaffer/other/sp/abb.htm

McCoy, A. W. (1991). *The Politics of Heroin: CIA Complicity in the Global Drug Trade*. New York: Lawrenceville Books.

Mokdad, A. H., Marks, J. S., Stroup, D. F., & Gerberding, J. L. (2004). Actual causes of death in the United States, 2000. *Journal of the American Medical Association*, 291(10): 1238–1241.

Nordt, C., & Stohler, R. (2006). Incidence of heroin use in Zurich, Switzerland: a treatment case register analysis. *Lancet*, *367*: 1830–1834.

Paige, H. M., & Beck, A. J. (2006). *Prisoners in 2005*. US Department of Justice, Bureau of Justice Statistics, Washington, DC: US Department of Justice, November.

Pew Center on The States (2008). One in one hundred: behind bars in America. www.pewcenteronthestates.org/uploadedFiles/8015 PCTS_prison08_FINAL_2-1-1_FORWEB.pdf.

Robinson, M. B., & Scherlen, R. (2007). *Lies, Damned Lies, and Drug War Statistics: A Critical Analysis of Claims Made by the Office of National Drug Control Policy*. New York: State University of New York Press.

SAMHSA (Substance Abuse and Mental Health Services Administration) (1999). *National Household Survey on Drug Abuse: Summary Report 1998*. Rockville, MD: Substance Abuse and Mental Health Services Administration.

Siegel, R. K. (1989). *Intoxication: Life in Pursuit of Artificial Paradise*. New York: E. P. Dutton.

Shepard, E. (2002). We wasted billions on DARE. *The Education Issue: ReconsiDer Quarterly*, *1*(4): 1–11.

Stossel, J. (2002). War on drugs, a war on ourselves. *ABC News* Television Special, New York, 30 July.

US Census Bureau (2007). Total male slaves in United States in 1840 numbered 1,244,384. Geospacial and Statistical Data Center, University of Virginia Library, http://fisher.lib.virginia.edu/cgi-local/censusbin/census/cen.pl, accessed 22 July 2007.

US Census Bureau, Population Division (2003). www.census.gov/main/www/popclock.html, accessed 8 July 2003.

Van Bakel, R. (2002). End the drug war now! *Maxim Magazine*, February.

Walmsley, R. (2003). *World Prison Population List* (4th edn). London: Home Office Research, Development and Statistics Directorate. www.homeoffice.gov.uk/rds/pdfs2/r188.pdf, (accessed 29 April 2003).

PART III

STRATEGIES FOR ENABLING CHANGE

CHAPTER EIGHT

Human security and conflict

Jennifer Leaning

Introduction

The argument advanced in this chapter is that human security, the essential social expression of human attachment, is at once highly vulnerable to the ravages of war and tightly linked to all efforts to prevent and mitigate its effects. The build-up to war is often influenced by erosion of human security. The period during the war may be marked by sustained assaults on human security, particularly if the warring parties make no effort to limit harmful effects on civilians. The period of transition out of war is a particularly pivotal time in which attention to issues of human security may promote or degrade efforts at stabilization and recovery. It is argued here that recognition of the pivotal role that human security plays during pre-, intra-, and post-conflict periods is foundational to local, national, and international policies that seek to prevent war, mitigate conflict, and help post-war societies to recover.

This argument is based on empirical and theoretical strands from the social sciences, history, psychology, public health, and international law. It is buttressed and supported by data gathered from contemporary settings and by informed observation of recent and current conflict and post-conflict settings.

Human security

The notion of human security arises from an analysis of the world that establishes people, rather than nation-states, as the central repositories of value, meaning, and authority. The roots of this analysis can be traced to the early days of the Enlightenment (Rothschild, 1995). The notion surfaced in international policy deliberations with the 1983 Palme Report, *Common Security*, which argued that the nuclear arms race missed the point, that the real security of the world rested on whether people themselves, in every country, felt that their own social, economic, and political needs were being met (Independent Commission on Disarmament and Security Issues, 1982). Human security, as a term and as an aspiration, received prominent attention in the 1994 UN Development Report (United Nations Development Programme, 1994) and has been extensively explored in the scholarly and policy literature that provided momentum for the international effort that in 2003 produced the UN-sponsored Human Security Report (Commission on Human Security, 2003). The wide-ranging essays in this last report establish through empirical and theoretical discussion that governments and the international community must shift from a dominant emphasis on accumulation of arms and elaboration of international political arrangements to efforts that strengthen the foundations of livelihoods and social enterprise that make people healthy and comfortable within their own communities and regions.

The concept of human security invoked here is tightly linked to this discussion. It moves the focus more intensely to the psychosocial dynamics of individuals and communities, and looks in particular at these dynamics in societies in transition from oppression or conflict. This focus is based on the recognition that human beings share common psycho-social needs of identity, recognition, participation, and autonomy (Amoo, 1997). These human needs obtain regardless of economic status or political stability, but are muted or submerged when people are in absolutely desperate circumstances, such as in the immediate settings of famine or gross physical insecurity. Once minimum survival needs have been met, however, these needs will surface and demand engagement. People will seek to be seen for who they are, will need to feel that they belong, will ask to be heard, and will begin to make claims and assert agency. These dynamics, which can be assessed at both the individual and community level, will exert enormous influence over the extent to which external assistance of any kind can be absorbed and integrated into the local setting to good effect. The case for this approach to human security was first advanced as an analytic guide to agencies engaged in post-conflict settlement and recovery activities (Leaning & Arie, 2001). That guide included a detailed discussion of metrics and means of assessing key components of human security.

The three main components of this concept of human security involve a sense of home, a link to community, and a positive sense of the future, or a sense of hope. The component of home captures many aspects of the human need to establish and maintain identity. Home harbours records and memories of interactions as well as sensations and feelings regarding attachment to a particular place. The concept of home may be forced into elasticity, however, as war or disaster forces people to leave their ancestral burial plots, their farms or villages, and the experience of a stable and dear landscape and night sky. The family unit, even in flight or exile, may provide the assurance and support that individuals need in order to maintain their sense of who they are and where they belong.

The component of community in this definition of human security includes the need to be recognized and to be able to participate in the larger world. The meaning of community coheres around relationships, some of which are based on personal relationships or extended kinship ties, but many of which are built through familiar, secure, and repeated interactions with a broad range of independent actors. To varying degrees, all people yearn to take part in such networks in order to meet their individual and family lists of needs, expectations, and desires. If land is to be bought or sold, a marriage to take place, food to be purchased or bartered, some form of community is required. The essential element in these relationships is impersonal trust, achieved through repetitive and predictable transactions. Communities built on homogenous identity lines, however, may prove antagonistic when facing outsiders, and communities built on established lines of wealth and class may prove fractious if sudden shifts in horizontal inequalities disturb long-held assumptions and stabilities. In the human security model advanced here, community is a fraught concept, filled with promise of social and economic diversity but also known to produce deadly animosities.

The human need for autonomy is captured in the stance towards the future. People with a positive sense of the future will strive to achieve a sense of agency through time, to construct their own future in ways that will expand their sense of well-being and capacity. People with a negative sense of the future will not make investments for the long term and may take high risks for short-term gain. Assessing this component of human security entails identifying aspects of hopefulness in behaviour or attitude, such as saving for educational expenses of children. In its negative mode, people may make decisions based on a high discount rate, where what appears to be destructive or wasteful behaviour may, in fact, derive from a profound sense of despair about what the future may hold.

This model of human security has great relevance to the approach that the international community takes to populations that have just emerged from war, oppression, or major disaster. Without an understanding of underlying dynamics of human security, it is possible to ask too much of people in the early phase, when they are bereft and lack a sense of home and belonging. It is possible to distribute resources in ways that aggravate underlying community hostilities or to flood a community with resources it cannot yet legitimately absorb and regulate. And it will be easy to dismiss high-risk behaviour as simply that, without realizing the lack of hope that lies behind it. Deploying the human security model involves assessing individuals and groups along these parameters of home, community, and sense of the future, and then adjusting the flow of inputs and expectations to meet people where they are, rather than where the international community might wish them to be.

Impact of war on human security

The immediate impact of war upon society is usually assessed in terms of numbers of military dead, numbers of civilians forced into flight, extent of infrastructure destroyed, and short-term economic costs. Estimates of civilian mortality in conventional wars and current intra-state wars are highly variable and speculative, always incomplete, and accomplished long after the fact, since no formal institution has ever been assigned responsibility for ongoing, contemporaneous enumeration of non-combatant deaths.

Longer-term impacts of war include an elaboration of these quantifiable elements (military mortality, forced migration, destruction of the built environment, and economic costs) along with discussion of less quantifiable factors such as destruction or contamination of the natural environment, longer-term economic effects, and social, political, and psychological consequences (Laquer, 1984). Enumerating these longer-term impacts often prove in themselves to be very drawn out inquiries. It may take decades before participants begin to write deeply and honestly about their memories of events and their views of what has been lost or gained. Even more years may transpire before archives are opened or retrieved and national census and accounting systems are developed or reinstated.

In many parts of the world, attempts to assess both short and longer-term impacts are severely hampered by the inadequacy of record keeping during the pre-war period and by the widespread destruction of records brought about by the war itself. During the conflict, and for months to years after the ceasefire, it may be that the only information available for understanding the situation of civilians derives from surveys conducted by humanitarian organizations and international institutions, such as the United Nations and the International Committee of the Red Cross.

The following brief review of the impact of war on human security examines social and psychological aspects that are not immediately or easily quantifiable. The extent of these negative qualitative consequences is directly related to the intensity and duration of what we might call a continuum of suffering, an imposition of loss, and a contribution to atrocity that is felt across all sectors of the population, combatant and non-combatant alike.

The burden of loss

Long and intense wars, particularly those associated with aerial bombardment or repeated ground assaults over the same terrain, cause great urban and environmental destruction. Vast stores of accumulated wealth, culture, and history disappear. Assessments by the US Strategic Bombing Survey of war damage in Germany (1945), and in Japan (US Strategic bombing Survey, Pacific War, 1946) contain estimates of numbers of destroyed buildings and major structures, but do not convey the sweeping loss of centuries of recorded and constructed products of civilized activity (libraries, museums, religious structures, gardens, archives, statues).

The reconstruction process creates its own pattern of new wealth and new debt, whether it is supported by the victors (as in post-war Europe and Japan) or it is not (as in the USSR). But many things and places cannot be recreated or replaced. And the list of what has been lost is always incomplete.

For example, no accounting has ever been done of the impact of the 1991–1992 shelling of Mogadishu. This beautiful and urbane coastal city, resplendent in flowering shrubs and trees, abundant in restaurants and cultural sites reflecting an Italian gloss on centuries of Arab and African commerce, was utterly and pitifully transformed in the space of three punishing months to a rubble-filled landscape of concrete and sand, stripped of all services, devoid of capacity for social life. Fifteen years later, the nation is still in chaos and the city a squalid jumble of *ad hoc* settlements and minimal amenities.

A more recent example of the impact of long and intense conflict can be seen in Afghanistan in 2001, as it emerged from twenty-three years of fighting first the Soviet invasion and then a civil war. Most of the irrigation and waterworks, virtually all of the bridges and tunnels, many of the roads, and large sections of the major cities were all damaged or destroyed. Explosive remnants of war dating from the start of the war with the Soviet Union were scattered throughout the countryside and the cities that saw heavy conflict. Latest estimates suggest that over four million people live in land-mine-affected areas (Fruchet & Kendellen, 2006). Of the estimated population of twenty million, over 20% (four million) were forced by the conflict to seek refuge in Iran, Pakistan, or elsewhere; another two million are estimated to have been displaced throughout the country. Between one and two million people are thought to have been killed. In late 2001 and early 2002, the cities were filled with people who had fled the conflict in rural areas. The alleys and edges of the streets were filled with makeshift shelters for the homeless and the beggars, many of them war widows, orphans, and amputees. The major museums and libraries had been sacked, the carefully cultivated gardens of the elite razed in the battles for different sections of the cities. The orchards and vineyards of the main agricultural lands had been cut down for firewood. Because of rural flight from the land, a severe three-year drought, and destruction of all built waterworks, agricultural production was at a minimum. Serious shortages of food and shelter were felt throughout the country.

The international community welcomes the occasion of a cease-fire, whenever and wherever it can be obtained. When the fighting is brought to a close, however, people emerge from shelters or return from afar to confront unremitting ugliness. The tidal disorder of war has obliterated the expected divide between construct and space, between settlement and nature. The eye cannot escape the rubble of buildings, the bombed-out streets, the sheer absence of everything. Huge holes and breaches in the ruins recall where treasured landmarks used to stand, even the rubble has been stripped of pipes and wires, glass, trim, and tyres. In the country-side, the paths and fields are littered with abandoned and stripped down tanks or jeeps. Forests are shorn, mountainsides gouged out, military forts and installations mar the horizons, and the earth is not safe to tread on for fear of mines and munitions.

It is a struggle for people to move past these sensory perceptions and the feelings they evoke. In Afghanistan, women and older men were particularly vocal about the waste that war had brought, the destruction of everything they had loved and that had given life meaning. They expressed strong anger at the men, including their own men, who had persisted in the madness of conflict over the previous two decades, and in this time had driven the country into something ghastly and decimated, a place from which they recoiled even as they had to remain (Holleufer, Leaning, & Briton, 2000).

These reactions echo ones that are only now being assembled, arising from the (now elderly) stunned citizens who gazed at the demolished cities and towns of post-war Germany. In the years that followed, as Sebald notes in accounts of these feelings, people repressed their bleak dismay and outrage, acquiescing to the sweep-ing world consensus that whatever had happened to Germany and the Germans was well deserved. Repression and denial were also necessary defences against the horrors of what people had seen and experienced. Yet, fifty years later, the emotional and cognitive reality of those times for the immediate survivors is finally beginning to surface (Sebald, 2003, pp. vii–x; 3–104).

Although we are beginning to note and even look for these feelings of dislocation and alienation as relevant aspects of the psychological costs of war, we have not yet formulated the ways to identify these feelings systematically on a population basis. Nor have we developed the methods to measure their relative influence, in terms of life choices and behaviour through time, for either individuals or groups.

The layered experience of loss in war includes the disruption and disorientation of flight and return. Flight from war may take people to distant havens where the culture and the environment are completely different from what is familiar and loved. Even forced dislocation to another part of one's country means leaving particular dwellings, gardens, landscapes, and burial grounds. In the immediate transition, when survival of oneself and one's family is at stake, forced migrants make do and accommodate. But, as time goes on and return either becomes impossible or becomes a trip back to a place that has ceased to exist except in memory, the sorrow at what cannot be recovered begins to seep in. We underestimate, at risk of missing immensely important aspects of human well-being, the extent to which human beings, even those in industrialized and urban societies, retain attachments to particular places.

This forced migration not only breaks the bonds that people have to their homes and their land, but leads to new and often alienated settlement upon return. When we look at countries where war was waged at least in part on their own territories, as in post-war Europe or Japan, or as in more recent conflicts, a consistent finding appears to be rapid and pronounced urbanization. In the Soviet Union, by 1961, sixteen years after the Second World War, the majority of the population had moved into urban areas (Judt, 2005, p. 385). It is estimated that post-war Angola has over 50% of its population in the coastal capital of Luanda (Jenkins, Robson, & Cain, 2002).

This urbanization does not necessarily reflect positive individual choice. Rural areas may be depopulated, mined, devoid of employment opportunities. Going to the cities is the only option, and to some a very unwelcome one, despite the surface bustle of international activity and new investment. Urban squatters in large towns in Angola dimly remember their farms, villages, and ancestral cemeteries, hundreds of miles in the interior, made inaccessible by years of war and rampage, now still out of reach because of landmines, unpassable roads, and economic ruin in the region. Afghan workmen, filling thin stoves with firewood for Kabul residents, grip thick cords of grapevine, remnants from vines that took 30–40 years to grow, and lapse back on their knees, recalling what life had been like when they were young, the grapevines standing, and the wars not begun.

War also imposes a set of demographic changes upon the surviving population. Most of these involve loss, as in physical and mental disability among veterans and affected civilians, loss of spirited and brave leaders (killed or forced into exile), and general attrition in labour force and skills, that comes from sheer population loss. For men, the intra-war mobilization of women into the workplace can be perceived as a loss, and when post-war societies reverse that gender shift, the return from the workplace to home can appear to be a loss for women. Much has been written about these issues, particularly in relation to the two major world wars of the twentieth century. It suffices to note that these demographic factors are at play as well in the less well studied internal and civil wars that have occurred since 1945.

The burden of atrocity

The breakdown of distinction between warrior and civilian, home front and battle front, characterizes many of the current non-state or intra-state conflicts. This breakdown of distinction has also occurred in many so-called conventional wars, past and present, at different phases of these wars and in different locations where they have been waged.

Conflict analysts who note this loss of definitive boundary between civilians and combatants in past or current wars agree that the causes are multiple but emphasize different factors as major determinants (Kaldor, 2007). In the major conventional wars of the twentieth century, atrocity-laden campaigns against civilians are seen as arising from formal command authorization or in the final stages of long and brutal struggles, where command authority had broken down or dissipated under the stress of events. In current intra-state wars, or in the case of insurgencies launched within nation-state wars (Iraq, Afghanistan), some analysts cite lack of training or disciplined command structures among non-state armed groups who have not benefited from the indoctrination given to formal military forces. Others discern a deliberate disregard for doctrine of international humanitarian law, in service of a strategy that privileges assault on civilian populations. This assault in turn can spring from several motivations: the need to cause people to flee and empty the land, because without supply lines and communication systems these armed groups cannot secure and hold a populated area; or the direct animus of ethnic cleansing, wherein the aim is not the capture of territory but the expulsion of stigmatized peoples. In the years since 11 September 2001, some analysts of trans-national groups describe the tactics of terror based on tenets of radical Islam, according to which the killing of those deemed infidels is not a transgression of international norms but a duty of the truly faithful. Other analysts emphasize the dynamics of asymmetric warfare, where, unless non-state actors break the rules of distinction, they face overwhelming odds against the military forces of modern states equipped with high-tech weapons in an electronic battlefield.

It is possible that wars with the most destructive effects on human security are those where bounds between civilian and combatant status are not drawn or are consistently violated. Home is invaded, community torn asunder, the future marred by guilt, anger, loss, and fear. In these wars, where communities are split along communal lines (race, religion, language, ethnicity), individuals and groups targeted on the basis of their communal characteristics are forced to undergo a profound disorientation in their sense of social stability, trust, and personal identity. For the targets of attack, what once seemed safe and taken for granted (a neighbour's smile, a courtesy at the market) turns into a lethal connection. To be recognized is to be at risk. The foundations of one's world slip away.

Wars laced with atrocity consume much social capital. Large numbers of people, victims and perpetrators, find it difficult to resume their lives for years after the ceasefires and peace accords. Guilt, humiliation, fear, rage, denial, and rejection may haunt the perpetrators. The victims carry their own versions of these feelings. Talent and energy are drained from the post-war project of reconstruction.

The feelings and memories may find other avenues of expression. Analysts speak of the "trauma story," a communal construct of what happened and what may lie ahead (Volkan & Itzkowitz, 1994, pp. 7–10). This story is tied to experience but elaborated to confer meaning, explanation, and exculpation for the side that tells and conveys it. Often these stories are mirror images of each other, one told by the perceived victim (but perhaps perpetrator to the other), the other told from the other point of view. The traumatic event may lurk in past centuries (for modern Serbs and Kosovar Albanians it is the 1389 Battle on the Field of Blackbirds) or in recent history (for India and Pakistan, it is the 1947 Partition; for radical anti-US Islamists it is the first Gulf War). Regardless, the trauma story serves to drive a wedge between communally defined groups and to freeze-frame their interpretation of all subsequent events.

Hence, human security may remain out of reach for generations.

Human security and policies relating to conflict

Pre-conflict situations

Despite significant advances in the scholarly and policy communities, the characterization of a society as entering a "pre-conflict phase" has proved to be troublesome. Indicators of early warning can identify societies that are at risk but have not been shown to have marked predictive power (International Commission on Intervention and State Sovereignty, 2001, p. 21). However, sufficient work has been done, by economists and political scientists in particular, to suggest that the human security concept has real theoretical and policy application to efforts at identification of risk and stabilization of trends.

The human security concept asks that we focus on individual capacities and human life, in the context of promoting an individual's active engagement with networks of support and communication. Human security, thus, rests on certain types of capacities and capabilities that successfully support group resilience and coping. These constructive attachments need not just be co-operative—in fact, many of the most successful are those that enhance competition. Certain kinds of rivalries (markets, democratic elections, for instance) are healthy components of a society whose individuals feel grounded at home, equipped to be at ease in their communities, and at least moderately confident of their future.

The challenge in pre-war settings is to identify those destructive tensions and attachments that lead to conflict, rather than to productively co-operative or competitive social behaviours. This challenge requires attention to three questions: what are the tensions that can be seen as de-stabilizing; what changes in the environment, circumstances, or relationships will introduce or aggravate these tensions; and, finally, what different groups are likely to be involved, or coalesce, in relationship to these tensions. In other words, who will stand to win or lose with regard to exogenous or endogenous change?

Many of these societies that engender "pre-conflict" scrutiny are very poor and among the world's most vulnerable (in terms of withstanding economic or political shocks). They are struggling to educate growing numbers of young people and find ways to integrate them into stagnant or collapsing economies. This demographic "youth bulge" is often referenced as a source of human insecurity and a risk factor for future war (Goldstone, 2001). Other societies in this risk category, however, may lie in the more middle range of the human development index but contain within them traditions of hierarchy, discrimination, and social exclusion that entrench a trajectory of economic growth and power for only the elite, or only a few groups. Both categories of societies are likely to suffer from an absent or insufficiently developed set of regulatory and administrative systems that apply equally and fairly to all members of the society. Even if a modicum of material goods is available, there may be major and dysfunctional gaps in the way these societies have adopted the rule of law.

These anticipatory assessments of vulnerabilities, risk, and resilience are necessary to make when granting aid, introducing development strategies, or supporting existing leaders and power structures (Collier et al., 2003). Human rights abuses have human security implications and ill-advised measures intended to shore up human security can badly backfire. Infusion of resources with the aim of promoting human security (schools, health care, roads, investment and market opportunities) may differentially benefit those who already hold power or status and thus intensify or solidify discriminatory or abusive structures and behaviours. This added burden on the vulnerable or marginalized may accelerate their growing sense of human insecurity.

Informed attention to home, community, and sense of the future—the human security perspective—invokes issues of dignity, equity, and voice. What conditions and fears do excluded groups express or experience? What instances of direct or indirect harm have occurred to certain groups in these societies that can be examined in terms of harbingers of potential trends and escalations? Here is where a close reading of competing communal narratives becomes most valuable. Grievances from past conflicts, especially those that have pitted groups within a society against each other or have engaged communal identities across nation-states, can be sustained for decades and even centuries. These sustained fault lines, if not deftly and directly addressed during times of relative stability, will provide fissionable material in times of crisis or rapid change. Hence, human security policies in the pre-conflict period must aim to support training and diffusion through all sectors of society, including the military, in the norms of human rights and international humanitarian law.

An indicator of risk of future conflict is whether the society has recently already been involved in war (Harff, 2003). Although this indicator is derived from a macro political analysis of large datasets, it could be argued that much of its empirical validity is rooted in the psychological dynamics of human insecurity. This indicator also reflects the historical finding that wars based on communal dynamics or ancient grievances can last for a very long time, exhaust material and human assets, and give rise in the post-conflict period to pervasive violence, humiliation, and annihilation of community self-respect. These wars are very difficult to recover from. For these reasons, an important aspect of human security strategy in the pre-conflict period is to maintain a high priority on policies aimed explicitly at conflict prevention and conflict mitigation.

The human security perspective, in the pre-conflict situation, thus suggests a mix of promotional and restraining strategies. Positive strategies include those that promote individual and group attachment to constructive activities of co-operation or competition. Negative strategies are those that reduce, block, or restrain the introduction or development of destructive group attachments.

It is outside the scope of this chapter to address the many examples of efforts that have been made in the field of conflict prevention. Successful use of preventive diplomacy, including deployment of preventive forces, took place when the international community intervened during the 1990s to restrain mass violence in Burundi and to forestall the spread of the Yugoslav conflict into Macedonia (Gurr, 1996, pp. 130–132).

Conflict situations

The terrible impact of war on civilians and combatants can be mitigated by a range of measures that reduce brutality and atrocity, limit assaults on civilians, minimize destruction of civilian assets, and create strong disincentives for grave violations of international law (Jones & Cater, 2001; Leaning, Arie, Holleufer, & Bruderlein, 2003). These measures fall into several main categories: (1) training of formal and non-state militaries, to the extent access can be obtained, throughout the duration of the war; (2) tactical use of incentives and disincentives in securing compliance with IHL in the field setting; (3) monitoring and reporting of formal and informal military interactions with civilian populations; (4) maintaining human contact with the outside world by humanitarian aid; (5) application of international diplomatic (and, at the extreme) military force, with the aim of bringing about a rapid ceasefire; and (6) creation of deterrence effect through enforcement of judicial procedures at the state and international level against individuals alleged to have committed war crimes.

A wide range of state and non-state actors have roles to play in carrying out these various measures. The International Committee of the Red Cross is a crucial agent for the first four measures, the result of its assigned tradition of engagement with combatants on all sides and monitoring of the conduct of hostilities. To the extent that formal military from outside nations are involved, their behaviour and reporting functions have the potential to restrain unlawful acts on the part of non-state actors. Humanitarian and human rights NGOs serve a critical function by providing a normative and empathetic connection with the international community. The relatively small niche afforded in international humanitarian law for the delivery of relief supplies and medical aid also creates the opportunity to bear witness, report on the hardships and atrocities, and convey the message that the outside world cares about what is happening to the local, ordinary people trapped inside the cauldron of hostilities.

In recent wars of the 1990s, in the period between the collapse of the cold war and the launch of the war on terror, the humanitarian role in protecting civilians from harm proved particularly robust (Bruderlein & Leaning, 1999). The space for humanitarian action, the so-called humanitarian niche, expanded in the areas where the great powers left (the war zones of Angola, Mozambique, and Sudan) and where international forces were absent, late, or ineffective (the conflicts in Somalia, Bosnia, Rwanda, and Kosovo). (The tragedy for Chechnya is that it was held in thrall by US–Russian relations during this period. For political and military reasons, the conflict was consigned by the international community to the Russian sphere of influence, and, in the anarchy of the first war [1994–1996], became a no-go zone for international humanitarian involvement.) During these years, humanitarian NGOs, working with the humanitarian agencies of the UN and the ICRC to build upon their collective experience from the 1980s response to famine and disaster, established a reasonably coherent approach to the support of refugees and internally displaced people in war-torn areas. This approach, at its best, gave practical life to the key tenets of international law. Weapons were not allowed in hospital zones and clinic areas, refugee camps were disarmed, medical personnel were trained, and health care protocols were developed. Attention to human rights and individual dignity began to thread through programmes, so that best practices were designed to reduce and respond to gender-based violence, broad-gauged psycho-social support programmes were introduced when settlements were considered sufficiently safe, and activities to promote child welfare and education became part of the standard mix of services in the more stable areas.

Much effective action can also be taken from outside the conflict zone on the part of civil society actors working with their own governments and the international community. Mobilizing grass-roots and elite demands for international diplomatic engagement (in terms of UN resolutions and public and private state communications) may prove influential (as it did in Somalia, Bosnia, Kosovo, and South Sudan). The content and tone of this diplomatic engagement are pivotal, in that carrots as well as sticks should be imaginatively entertained. Whatever measures are considered, their application needs to be specific and targeted, since non-state armed groups are less vulnerable to state-based sanctions but can be reached through pressure or positive incentives directed at the nation-states who grant these groups resources, sanctuary, and political support.

The threat of prosecution for war crimes may have marked deterrence effect if that threat can be carried out in a practical human time frame. Meeting that condition requires adequate funding and staffing of the International Criminal Court and sustained political support for this level of resource commitment on the part of the international community. It also requires that nation-states invigorate their own domestic law to create obligatory channels of co-operation and compliance (Ratner & Bischoff, 2004).

In the abstract, it is straightforward to argue that such measures, if implemented, could be seen to help sustain human security in war. Home, in terms of attachment to family and place, is central to the human security concept. In war, if the distinction between civilian and combatant has broken down or been deliberately discarded, home becomes one of the first targets. Community is crushed when war breaks out and pits identifiable groups and individuals, previously linked in forms of social networks, against one another. The notion of community turns ever more terrifying, however, when it becomes evident that people and groups whom one had trusted turn out to betray that trust in violent and vicious attacks on oneself and one's family. And, for all but the few who celebrate its onset, war blocks all paths to previously envisioned futures. It forces a confrontation with the present or a retreat into the past. The urgency of survival drains the capacity to dream. The longer the war continues, and the more extensive its destruction of beloved built structures, repositories of cultural memory, and treasured landscapes and vistas, the more alienated the population becomes from its future life in that terrain. A positive sense of the past carries people into the future. When that past is obliterated and its landmarks are gone, the future becomes a far more uncertain place.

But, in practical terms, the record is incomplete when it comes to assessing whether or not the particular measures discussed above have been shown to make much difference on the ground, for a given specific conflict. Seasoned humanitarian aid officers, policy makers, and academics have their own long list of positive anecdotes, even narratives and analyses (for example, see Kennedy, 2004; Minear, 2002; Rieff, 2002; Terry, 2002). What is inescapably evident to those who have witnessed war and efforts to mitigate its effects is that for some people, for some time, these forms of support and intervention have made a huge difference. Perhaps that is as much as can be hoped for. War is a terrible enterprise for all involved and efforts to diminish its reach can, at best, be accomplished only at the margins.

Post-conflict situations

A critical fallacy in thinking about war is to assume that when a ceasefire has taken place the war is then "over". The English language reinforces this error by providing few alternatives to words and phrases like "post-conflict", "post-war", "aftermath", "reconstruction", "recovery", "rehabilitation", "demobilization", "disarmament", "de-mining". At least the word "de-mining" is a gerund, connoting a sense of process and ongoing action.

The reality of war is that the immediate period after the ceasefire contains all the embers for a future rekindling of violent hostilities. An uncertainty characterizes this period, for which no working definition exists. Descriptive characteristics of this phase, which usually extends for weeks or months after the ceasefire agreement, include the fact that open fighting has ceased, there is some appreciable improvement in civilian security, and local leadership is starting to emerge. Spontaneous refugee return is beginning, people are already flocking to the cities to find work with the international humanitarian and peace-keeping agencies, and prices for food, housing, and petrol are beginning to soar.

The situation, depending upon the nature of the preceding war, is marked by mass population dislocation, high levels of insecurity for the population, possibly high levels of insecurity for members of the international community and those who work for them, widespread destruction of infrastructure, and a burden of unaddressed loss and atrocity (Médecins sans Frontières, 1997).

The overall goal for the local leadership and for the international community must be to agree upon the objectives of the stabilization and reconstruction efforts and the strategy for achieving them. A human security perspective would suggest an inclusive and participatory approach oriented towards restitution of safety, livelihoods, and local empowerment (World Bank, 1998).

That said, the threat of reversion to violence is very high in this early period and, regardless of process, a set of essential early measures must be quickly put into motion, in a sequence that attends to the psychological dynamics of the people and their leaders. In actuality, many of these measures are not introduced when needed or in proper sequence, and the grey time between war and peace, the post-conflict "transition" period (in USAID parlance), often extends into years.

These essential measures begin with shoring up security, an operational imperative but also extremely important from the human security perspective. People need to feel safe before they can begin to seek out steps back to a semblance of normal life. The main threats to security in the immediate post-ceasefire period are from armed groups, criminal elements, and weapons dispersed among members of the general population. Military or police forces must be deployed to maintain weapons-free civilian zones, guard public buildings and sites where resources are stored, organize traffic flows, and patrol streets and highways. Local or international police are usually more tolerated by the general population than military units and usually have the more appropriate training to maintain law and order. The task of disarming armed groups and collecting weapons from members of the public often requires months and should proceed under the command of the military, as part of the extended ceasefire and subsequent peace agreement.

As soon as physical insecurity has been reduced to a tolerable level, the authorities should proceed to provide basic human survival needs to the general civilian population (water, shelter, food, essential medical care). In this process, particular attention must be given to the protection and care of those populations that are most vulnerable. These populations will vary depending on the war context but usually include orphans, widows, amputees and other physically disabled people, and stigmatized groups at risk of reprisal or hostile attack.

The next steps that must be accomplished in a matter of months are almost all measures that derive from and reinforce a human security model.

First, policies relating to refugee and IDP return can either fully support the human security concept of home or rapidly vitiate it. Family tracing and reunification must be a priority. Giving people goods, seeds, and tools will be helpful, but attention must also be carefully tuned to issues of coping mechanisms and capacity building. During these first few months, the authorities and relief workers must recognize that the majority of people are not likely to be especially good at problem-solving, taking the initiative, or self-mobilization. Their entire fund of emotional and cognitive energy will be expended in the daily struggle for survival, adjusting to shifting and often alien circumstances, accommodating new or changed returnees, and managing their own feelings and memories.

An important factor in refugee and IDP return is the extent to which the land they left can readily be reclaimed. In many post-war situations, records have been lost or were based only on face-to-face witnessing and oral contracts. In the years since people fled, others may have moved in. Usually there are issues relating to the rights of widows to use, inherit, or transfer land. This question of land tenure becomes more bitter and complex the longer the conflict has gone on (as in Afghanistan, South Sudan, and Angola) and can be complicated, not improved, by government policies on land redistribution and relative de-mining priorities attached to commercial *vs.* subsistence land holdings (as in Angola).

Second, de-mining, notwithstanding the social competition behind identification of priority areas, is a critical element in creating a stable sense of home. It is well accepted that people will either not return or not return as large family groups if landmines or unexploded ordnance (explosive remnants of war, ERW) are known to exist in their own family plots, along the customary paths and roads, and at key intersections and bridges. The risk profile of local people varies within and between countries, but it is also a well accepted fact that for people to return to their homes, at minimum their entire village and farming area must have all sites of ERW contamination identified and all places where people actually live, farm, and routinely travel must be thoroughly de-mined. One stray accident with animal or human consequences will set back resettlement for a considerable period of time.

Third, closely linked to de-mining operations is the effort to repair roads and bridges and set up some kind of phone system. These must also be high priority tasks in this post-ceasefire setting. The problems of transport and communication can appear completely disabling to all other actions that the international and local communities try to put into motion. One cannot get to outlying areas to assess problems or deliver services. One cannot meet with people in nearby locales because travel times are extremely long (hours to days) and very unpredictable (traffic jams, a new collapse in an unstable road bed). One cannot make phone calls. Mobility, of people and ideas, is essential to all aspects of planning and operations. In these months after the fighting has stopped, mobility turns out to be the major bottleneck.

From the human security perspective, this problem of mobility is central to the recreation of community. Local people need to come together in some form of meetings and other participatory processes to talk about their concerns, make short-term plans, and organize co-operative work projects, such as clearing rubble or restoring wells. Re-starting basic markets relies on people bringing goods or produce to sell and others coming forward to buy or barter. These activities of engagement require some form of predictable transport and interactive communications. The lack of traversable roads and communication systems similarly grind down efforts of the international community to encourage these local activities as well as carry out their own operations. Hours of time and gallons of petrol are wasted each day trying to drive from one town to another, or driving across towns to find out if someone is at home, in the office, somewhere else, or en route to the meeting that is now three hours late and has only one-third of expected participants. Those NGOs and international players that rely on radio communication can deliver brief and linear messages but, useful as this mode is, it is no substitute for face-to-face gatherings of people from different sectors and local groups.

Early post-conflict settings are famous for traffic jams, operational inefficiencies, high levels of frustration, and recurrent confusion and misunderstanding among all parties. These issues are often direct results of, or certainly aggravated by, the difficulties of getting roads and phones to work.

Fourth, an over-arching determinant of community attitude is the strategy and methods used for identifying needs and distributing resources. Health centres, schools, hospitals, administrative buildings, housing, and other essentials for community life will have been destroyed or substantially depleted. Whenever outside aid comes in to help with reconstruction at this phase, the potential for splitting groups within communities along hostile competitive lines must be anticipated, identified, and dealt with on a continuous basis. The task of seeking opinion and reaching out to different groups in an unfamiliar community via intermediaries and translators is time-consuming, hazardous, and essential (Anderson, 1999). Several factors, in addition to the difficulty of the task, conspire to reduce the likelihood that agencies will take it on. Everyone has a sense of urgency and everyone tries to respond to the pent-up impatience of all actors to see tangible improvements in a very short time frame. In the rush to accomplish something tangible, this important task of assessing and dealing with fissiparous community dynamics often gets pushed aside.

Fifth, in the longer run, those in charge of the reconstruction process must make every effort to introduce some administrative regularity into the functions of daily life. These administrative structures serve at the local level to create the rudimentary elements of the rule of law: complaint procedures, detention centres, consistent definition and implementation of sanctions and punishments, requirements regarding commercial and banking transactions, some form of legitimate adjudication system. These structures will support a constructive pattern of individual and group behaviour and allow a productive mix of social and economic activities to take hold.

Then, throughout these early days and months, the authorities and the humanitarian community must remain alert to underlying psychological dynamics in the civilian population. Beneath the surface people will be dealing with feelings of guilt, anger, humiliation, and revenge. Families will be struggling to integrate members who have been away for years; returning neighbours may view each other with suspicion or outright certainty of previous atrocity. Social and legal processes for dealing with serious abuses committed during the conflict will not have been defined or set up during this period, leaving it up to local communities how they might deal with identified or suspected perpetrators. These concerns, if not dealt with as soon as is possible in a coherent, transparent, and participatory mode, will prove destructive to the longer-term re-knitting of community attachment and development of forward momentum towards the future.

Examples of successful human security strategies in this context include the vigorous de-mining efforts in Angola, which provide a sense of physical security and safety to the population, employ local people, and open up land for resettlement, and extensive road and bridge reconstruction in Kosovo, which supported a return to intra-country commerce and communication. Save the Children UK has launched a global effort to provide education to the estimated thirty-nine million conflict-affected children who have had their schooling severely disrupted by years of war and forced migration. Their recent report notes considerable progress in enlisting children and promoting stability and well-being in their school programmes (Save the Children UK, 2007).

This section on post-conflict policy has focused on the first weeks and months of international and local activity. If the measures outlined above are introduced in a timely and reasonably effective manner, the potential for the longer-term work, including local capacity building (Smillie, 2001) and conflict resolution (Byrne & Irvin, 2000), appears much greater. However, clambering out of war takes much longer, on a human scale, than descending into it. In many ways, Europe and parts of Asia are still dealing with the repercussions and consequences of the Second World War. It is not difficult to identify the themes in US social and political life that date directly from the Vietnam War, or, arguably, from the USA's Civil War of the mid-nineteenth century.

Conclusion

At the geopolitical level, there may be a warrant for some wars, at some times. A human security perspective, however, describes war as an almost generic process of calamitous damage and imperfect repair. Every war is different, yet each yields, to those who look for it, a recognizable pattern of human attachment and loss. At each juncture, in the turning towards war, in the midst of war, and in the final turning away, there are opportunities to enhance the attachment and mitigate the loss. We must acknowledge, however, that whatever might be done in these modes, there is always a negative balance. War takes away more than can be given back

References

Amoo, S. (1997). *The Challenges of Ethnicity and Conflicts in Africa: the Need for a New Paradigm.* UNDP Emergency Response Division. New York: United Nations.

Anderson, M. B. (1999). *Do No Harm: How Aid Can Support Peace—or War.* Boulder, CO: Lynne Reinner.

Bruderlein, C., & Leaning, J. (1999). New challenges for humanitarian protection. *British Medical Journal, 319*: 430–435.

Byrne, S., & Irvin, C. L. (Eds.) (2000). *Reconcilable Differences: Turning Points in Ethno-Political Conflict.* Bloomfield, CT: Kumarian.

Collier, P., Elliott, V. L., Hegre, H., Hoeffler, A., Reynal-Querol, M., & Sambanis, N. (2003). *Breaking the Conflict Trap: Civil War and Development Policy.* Washington, DC: World Bank and Oxford University Press.

Commission on Human Security (2003). *Human Security Now.* New York: Communications Development.

Fruchet, P., & Kendellen, M. (2006). *Landmine Impact Survey of Afghanistan: Results and Implications for Planning.* http://maic.jmu.edu/journal/9.2/focus/fruchet/fruchet.html (accessed 7 March 2006).

Goldstone, J. A. (2001). Demography, environment and security: an overview. In: M. Weiner & S. S. Russell (Eds.), *Demography and National Security* (pp. 38–61). New York: Berghahn Books.

Gurr, T. R. (1996). Early-warning systems: from surveillance to assessment to action. In: K. M. Cahill (Ed.), *Preventive Diplomacy: Stopping Wars Before They Start* (pp. 243–262). New York: Basic Books.

Harff, B. (2003). No lessons learned since the Holocaust? Assessing risks of genocide and political mass murder since 1955. *American Political Science Review, 97*: 57–73.

Holleufer, G., Leaning, J., & Briton, N. (2000). Unpublished report to the ICRC on the people on war project. Afghanistan country report. Boston: Harvard School of Public Health.

Independent Commission on Disarmament and Security Issues (1982). *Common Security: A Blueprint for Survival.* New York: Simon and Shuster.

International Commission on Intervention and State Sovereignty (2001). *The Responsibility to Protect.* Ottawa, Canada: International Development Research Centre.

Jenkins, P., Robson, A., & Cain, J. (2002). Local responses to globalization and peripheralization in Luanda, Angola. *Environment and Urbanization, 14*: 115–127.

Jones, B. D., & Cater, C. K. (2001). From chaos to coherence? Toward a regime for protecting civilians in war. In: S. Chesterman (Ed.), *Civilians in War* (pp. 237–262). Boulder, CO: Lynne Rienner.

Judt, T. (2005). *Postwar: A History of Europe Since 1945.* London: Penguin.

Kaldor, M. (2007). *New and Old Wars: Organized Violence in a Global Era* (2nd edn). Palo Alto, CA: Stanford University Press.

Kennedy, D. (2004). *The Dark Sides of Virtue: Reassessing International Humanitarianism.* Princeton, NJ: Princeton University Press.

Laquer, W. (1984). *Europe Since Hitler: The Rebirth of Europe.* New York: Penguin.

Leaning, J., & Arie, S. (2001). Human security: a framework for assessment in conflict and transition. *Working Paper Series, 11*(8). Cambridge, MA: Harvard Center for Population and Development Studies.

Leaning, J., Arie, S., Holleufer, G., & Bruderlein, C. (2003). Human security and conflict: a comprehensive approach. In: L. Chen, J. Leaning, & V. Narasimhan (Eds.), *Global Health Challenges for Human Security* (pp. 13–30). Global Equity Initiative, Harvard University. Cambridge, MA: Harvard University Press.

Médecins sans Frontières (1997). *World in Crisis: the Politics of Survival at the End of the Twentieth Century.* London: Routledge.

Minear, L. (2002). *The Humanitarian Enterprise: Dilemmas and Discoveries.* Bloomfield, CT: Kumarian.

Ratner, S. R., & Bischoff, J. L. (Eds.) (2004). International war crimes trials: making a difference. *Proceedings of an International Conference at University of Texas School of Law* (Nov 6–7, 2003). Austin: University of Texas.

Rieff, D. (2002). *A Bed for the Night: Humanitarianism in Crisis.* New York: Simon and Schuster.

Rothschild, E. (1995). What is security? *Daedalus, 124*: 53–98.

Save the Children UK (2007). Rewrite the future—one year on. www. savethechildren.org.uk/en/docs/rtf-oneyearon.pdf.

Sebald, W. G. (2003). *On the Natural History of Destruction*. New York: Random House.

Smillie, I. (Ed.) (2001). *Patronage or Partnership: Local Capacity Building in Humanitarian Crises*. Bloomfield, CT: Kumarian.

Terry, F. (2002). *Condemned to Repeat? The Paradox of Humanitarian Action*. Ithaca, NY: Cornell University Press.

United Nations Development Programme (1994). *Human Development Report*. New York: United Nations.

United States Strategic Bombing Survey (1945). *Summary Report, European War, September 30*: 15. http://www.anesi.com/ussbs02.htm

United States Strategic Bombing Survey (1946). *Summary Report, Pacific War, 1st July*. Washington, DC: United States Government Printing Office.

Volkan, V. D., & Itzkowitz, N. (1994). *Turks and Greeks: Neighbours in Conflict*. Huntingdon: Eothen Press.

World Bank (1998). *Post-Conflict Reconstruction: the Role of the World Bank*. Washington, DC: The World Bank.

CHAPTER NINE

Enabling change

Joan Woodward

The case for understanding the vital need for "secure attach-ment" in babies and young children as a basis for their sound development and good mental health has now been so well made that it no longer needs to be elaborated here, as an introduction to this chapter.

But how is it for us as adults? Whatever kind of attachments we have had, "secure" or "insecure", in our early life, we continue to seek secure attachments throughout our lives. The way we do this depends largely on our earlier "attachment history". Dr John Bowlby insists that the need for attachment is an "instinctive behav-iour" that exists in all of us as human beings "from the cradle to the grave" (Bowlby, 1998, p. 62). I believe this to be a fundamental truth, for I watch people constantly seeking secure attachment at every age. Sometimes, people who have had very insecure attach-ments in their early life will appear to run away from close connec-tion with anyone, but this is because they deeply fear once again experiencing rejection at an unbearable level. It does not mean that they have stopped longing for it.

The interesting questions are how and why our civilized Western societies have developed so many powerful institutions and organizations that not only deny these needs, but in many instances actively work against their being met. I have spent most of my professional life trying, in different fields, to get greater recognition of the importance of attachments that provide security. In the process, I have inevitably had to grapple with a variety of resistances to change. Before I move on to share some of these experiences, it seems important to describe the common elements of secure attachment that we seek throughout life and to examine the forces at work in society that strongly reject these elements even being recognized, let alone properly valued for the vital role that they play in our lives.

Secure attachments through the life cycle

Following many years of observation, Bowlby was able to recognize that the seeking of attachment is vital for babies and young children for their *actual survival*. He defines four essential elements of attachment that lead to a sense of security. The first is that the attachment figure (usually the mother in the beginning) is *available*. For babies and young children, this availability needs to be consistent and reliable. Bowlby was able to observe that for an eighteen-month-old child, when its mother leaves the room she has "gone", and many children will show distress in this situation. As the child grows and more understanding comes with it, by the age of three years most children can feel secure in the absence of their primary attachment figure, provided they know her whereabouts. For example, a child of that age can understand that mum has gone shopping, but will be back for lunch. This is because most children around that age can hold the mother figure in mind as someone who will come back. This availability of their primary attachment figure is particularly sought if the child is ill, tired, or upset. Adults, too, need more support at times when they feel more vulnerable. Most people suffer severe emotional distress when their marriage or a partnership breaks up, or even if these are threatened. The sense of loss when death of a spouse or partner occurs can feel overwhelming.

Bowlby described the second essential component of attachment that provides a sense of security as *responsiveness*. This is a complicated matter, because how a parent responds to the emotional needs of a young baby is utterly different from how they need to respond to an adolescent. For children, an attachment figure may be present and apparently physically available, but if their responses are inappropriate, ranging from non-response to one that is very inconsistent, or, worst of all, violent, then extreme feelings of insecurity can result.

For adults whose spouses, close partners, friends, or colleagues behave in these ways there is also likely to be a reaction of insecurity. For most people, their responses to such behaviours will be largely determined according to their earlier attachment experiences. They may become angry, withdraw, or become depressed. Sadly, many marriages are unhappy or flounder because so many men find it hard to express their feelings and to be fully responsive to their wives' or their children's emotional needs. Men traditionally have been brought up to believe that expressing feelings is equated with weakness.

The third important element Bowlby observed in attachment behaviour is that it *operates in a hierarchical way*. That is to say, we all know from babyhood who our primary attachment figure is. After that particular person (who is always the most important person in our lives) we may have a number of attachment figures that matter to us, grading to a lesser degree. Most of us can name four or five such people. Our attachment figures obviously change as we go through life. It is likely that one of our parents remains as the primary one until we become adult and find a partner or close friend. If, later in life, our partner dies, we may feel that one of our grown-up children takes over the primary role, or it may be a sibling or a person particularly close to us. Bowlby described how, for some people, their primary attachment may be some dominant figure such as an employer or some elder in the community (Bowlby, 1979, p. 87).

The fourth and very important element in attachments that provide us with feelings of security is that of *mutuality*. Most mothers seek and get pleasure from their babies' need of them. Frequently, mothers will describe how they are "in love" with their babies, rejoicing in the smile of recognition, enjoying cuddling and breast-feeding. The pleasures and rewards for both parties are *different*, but there is a sense of feeling both loved and valued by the other as the attachment deepens.

In suggesting the word "love" in a variety of forms, which in my view lies at the heart of attachments that make us feel secure, we immediately get a clue to the deeply embedded resistances and the strong forces at work in our society that oppose rather than promote such attachments.

I believe this is due to love being perceived as fundamentally subversive. Love—and the valuing this entails—challenges the power structures on which all our main institutions and organizations are based. This is because love is mutual and horizontal, whereas power structures are hierarchical and vertical. It is fear of the loss of this power that lies at the heart of all attempts to prevent those changes that could lead to a proper recognition of people's emotional needs and improve their sense of security. We have only to look at figures throughout history who have promoted love, from Christ to Martin Luther King to John Lennon, to see just how dangerous their messages have been perceived to be by those in power.

It seems important at this point to remind ourselves, so that we may never forget, just how brutal the powerful forces of the Establishment have been when resisting those who challenged them with their needs for attachment. For example, it is such a short time ago that men who loved other men were imprisoned as criminals for their sexual preferences. This changed in England in 1967, in Scotland in 1980, and it took two more years for it to change in Ireland. The "criminal" was then turned into a "psychiatric patient", which for many was an equally terrifying definition. (If they were no longer "bad" they were "mad".) It was not until 1973 that homosexuality was removed from the official List of Psychiatric Diagnoses by The American Psychiatric Association. The World Health Organisation followed suit in 1992. It took until 1993 for the UK government to do it. It is not surprising that the fall-out from this attitude to homosexuality still remains in many areas, particularly in the established church. Lesbians, too, have suffered from severe discrimination, though they were never actually criminalized.

In the 1950s, I observed a homosexual man being given "aversion therapy" in a psychiatric hospital in an attempt to make him change his sexual feelings. He received electric shocks from the arms of his chair as images were shown to him on a screen. Such "treatments" seem barbaric now, but were accepted well into the 1970s.

Similarly ruthless and barbaric was the brutal way women were force fed when on hunger strike in prison, having militantly demanded their right to vote. All they wanted was to be fully valued as human beings and recognized as citizens equal to men. Although women eventually gained the vote, at great cost for some, there are many areas even now, particularly in the "Establishment", where they are still not fully valued as equals to men. This is particularly true in some religious regimes, where the rules are determined by men, and is also clearly shown through pay differentials and the low number of women in all the high-ranking professions. My own grandfather, who was an influential surgeon, insisted that as women's brains weighed less than those of men they could not be as intelligent, and therefore must never train as doctors!

My own involvement in struggling with others to bring about changes also exposed some cruelty on the part of the powerful Establishment figures trying to resist them. I like to believe that this was largely due to ignorance, but I think that many of those who wield power are unaware of the deeper reasons for their difficulties in modifying, let alone relinquishing, their authority. I believe this is due to the difficulty many people have in facing the truth of their own attachment histories and the effect this has had on them. The next section begins with my experiences with children in hospital.

Changing care for children in hospital

One of the main areas where the emotional needs of children have finally come to be recognized is in hospitals. The difference between the way children are treated in hospital now and what used to happen forty years ago is evidence of one of the most successful lobbying movements. It originally faced incredibly strong opposition from a variety of entrenched forces. When examining how these changes were brought about, it is always interesting to look at how it started.

In 1961, I was asked to set up a branch in Birmingham of what was already called "Mother Care for Children in Hospital" (MCCH). This was largely due to my having just finished nearly five years' work at Birmingham Accident Hospital, during which time I had completed a research study into the emotional effect of burns on children (Woodward, 1959).

Some time earlier, a small group of mothers had fortuitously met on a bench in Battersea Park, in London. They all felt distress at having a child in a hospital that had very restricted visiting rules. They decided that something must be done about it. One of them knew my mother, who, as a journalist, was able to write a piece in the Women's page of the *Guardian* asking readers to support MCCH. The flood of responses showed that the desire for change among mothers was deeply felt and nationwide. A Head Office for MCCH was set up in London and gradually, over the following years, branches spread across the country. At this stage they consisted largely of mothers determined to persuade hospital administrators and medical staff to allow parents to stay in with young children and to offer open visiting hours for all children.

In 1953, Bowlby had written in a popular form his findings from a previous report he wrote for The World Health Organisation. He titled it *Child Care and The Growth of Love* (Bowlby, 1953). It produced a great deal of controversy. In the same year, James Robertson, a social worker who worked with Bowlby at The Tavistock Clinic, made a now famous film, *A Two-Year-Old Goes to Hospital*. This showed the effect of separation on the child. Later on, he made another film entitled *Going to Hospital with Mother*, and published a book to accompany it (Robertson, 1958). Four years later, he edited a very different sort of book; it was a compilation of letters from mothers about their harrowing experiences of having children in hospital, which had been collected by the *Observer* newspaper (Robertson, 1962). This book was invaluable for me, as I started my local campaign by lending out twenty-five copies of it to every family I knew who had young children, whether they had been in hospital or not.

I met an amazing amount of opposition to the idea that hospitals caring for children should be far more open to parents. The arguments against it, then, were that "doctors and nurses know best", that mothers would be a "nuisance", and there were some suggestions of a punitive kind with the implication that the mothering could not have been all that good if their child was in hospital! Fortunately, there was a far greater supportive response, and soon a small number of us formed a committee. We held our first big meeting in January 1963 and set up the Birmingham branch of MCCH. At the same time, many other branches were forming and being supported by the Head Office in London, with backing from a few progressive paediatricians.

I need to go back at this point to describe something of the research I did earlier, because it was that work that enabled me to understand not only the emotional needs of the children and their parents in a hospital setting, but also to recognize some of the causes of the resistances to these needs being met.

I look back with incredulity at how I took up the research post at the beginning of 1957 under the auspices of the Medical Research Council (MRC). Sometime earlier a technician had queried why the children in the burns unit seemed so distressed, and the question was raised as to whether burns caused emotional disturbance in children, or whether emotionally disturbed children got burned. In 1957 I had come to live in Birmingham, and the challenge of finding a reliable answer to these questions deeply interested me. I went on two visits to the hospital to discuss how such a study might be done and felt deeply dispirited as I was shown round the ward. It became quickly apparent that I would have to provide a detailed proposal myself.

When I arrived to start the study, there was no room, desk, or even telephone available for me and the appointment was limited to six months. I had suggested visiting the mothers to obtain an opinion on their children's emotional state, as they could compare how their child was both before and after the accident. The Director of the MRC defined burns to over 10% of the body area as correlating with clinical shock. He suggested that the visits should be made to the mothers of children who had been burned four to five years previously. This was because burns take a long time to heal and many children come back repeatedly for further skin grafts.

As I set out each day, I did not know what sort of reception I would get as a hospital representative. I hoped that I could get each mother to trust me enough to want to talk. The most common symptoms in the children that the mothers spoke about were a variety of specific fears such as the dark, being alone, or of people in white coats, resembling the doctors they remembered. Some of the children had generalized feelings of anxiety and others were withdrawn or lethargic. I was well aware that "disturbance" in children is largely a matter of opinion, but, as I listened to their mothers' stories, I was dismayed by the depth of their distress so long after their children's accidents. Sixteen per cent of the mothers had had a psychiatric referral, which they all put down to their reaction to their child's accident. As the mothers spoke with me, it became apparent that many had never had the opportunity to share their feelings with anyone in this way before.

By the fourth month I had visited ninety-nine families and received school reports, where relevant, in order to get further opinions on the emotional state of the children. I had asked the mothers about siblings' behaviour as well, to form some kind of control group.

My first report was met with opposing responses from the Director of the MRC, and the consultant. One said it was "not formal enough' and the other that it was "too formal'"! In spite of this, I was asked to investigate another hundred families whose burns had occurred two and three years previously. This time, I was given three months in which to do it, as well as visiting a matched control group. Many of the children lived many miles away from the hospital, so I had a very demanding task ahead.

Subsequently, I was able to contribute the findings of the study to the Platt Report, *The Welfare of Children in Hospital* (1959). The *British Medical Journal* published two of my papers (Woodward, 1959, 1962), and the consultant and I had a shared paper published (Woodward & Jackson, 1961). When the research study was over, I was offered a contract to join the Social Work Department of the hospital where I was able to continue the work of supporting the parents on the wards and in the out-patient clinics, as well as making many home visits.

During the time of the research I was asked to observe and recommend to the consultant any changes I thought might be helpful. I pressed hard for all children to be given daily visits, as previously none of the under fives had any, unless they were very seriously ill. This was based on a widely held belief that parents visiting "made the children cry". Finally, after a meeting that exposed huge levels of opposition and involved the hospital matron, it was decided to allow daily visiting at 3 p.m. "for half an hour, when nothing officially was happening on the ward". I was astounded on going to the ward the next day to see nets put up over the cots to make sure no mother lifted out or touched her child!

On one occasion a little later, a very articulate small boy, aged four, asked me when his mother would come to visit him. When I said she could not come until the afternoon, not because she did not want to see him, but because of the hospital rules, he said, "But don't they *know* that when I'm poorly I need my mummy more?" I felt rendered as helpless as he was, and I thought that his words needed to be carved into every administrator's desk.

There were two factors that gradually helped visiting hours to be increased. The first was that the findings of the study showed that burns produced a very high degree of emotional disturbance in children and the lack of parental visiting to the under fives correlated with the highest levels of disturbance. The second was that the head pathologist had offered to monitor infection levels on the unit once visiting was increased to every day. This was because it was believed that parents on the ward would increase infection and this belief had been used for years as another reason for keeping out parents. The result of monitoring was cause for celebration, as the infection rate actually went down.

I continued to be involved for many years with MCCH (which then changed its name to The National Association for the Welfare of Children in Hospital—NAWCH). This enabled it to embrace professional members as well as parents. It soon became apparent that some mothers did not know how to cope with changes in their children's behaviour when they came home. I was able to write a small book with examples of problems and suggestions of how to understand them (Woodward, 1978). The influence of NAWCH continued to grow through many Annual Conferences. Strong pressures were brought to bear by the directors and chairwomen on individual hospitals as well as health authorities and the Department of Health. Many books were published about the issues involved, and local branch members made hundreds of persuasive visits to hospitals, raised funds, and produced all kinds of publicity. Play facilities were seen as of great importance too. The training of nurses was changed and, over a long period of time, attitudes have altered. Many young people today have no idea of the amount of hard work involved in bringing these changes about, as now parents take it for granted that they can stay in with their young children and that there will be open visiting, and play facilities in all hospitals for children.

Resistances to change

In attempting to analyse why it took so long for all these changes to come about, I believe it is necessary to examine why the opposition was so strong. I believe that the strongest resistance came from the doctors, nurses, and administrators, who were determined to keep in control of hospitals and their own wards in particular. They spread the belief that "doctors know best". They saw mothers as people who would "mess up" the ward or "be hysterical". Most of all, they perceived parents as people who might challenge the staff's power and control. They felt strongly that mothers should be "kept in their place", which was *outside the hospital*.

It is no wonder that mothers at that time felt intimidated when visiting, often fearful of talking to doctors and nurses. Many mothers expressed to me how inadequate and guilty they felt at "bothering staff". One of the reasons given so often for keeping mothers out was that their visits made the children cry. I believe this was based on the fact that where visiting had been allowed, it was in small slots of time and all the parents left at once, setting up an inevitable wail of desolation. Once visiting is open, parents can come and go and the atmosphere on the ward is very different.

One of the issues that was rarely aired was the feeling of jealousy on the part of some of the older nurses. Many of them had trained at times when married nurses were not accepted; they were single women whose lives were hard and who felt very possessive towards their small patients. They did not want to have any "interference by mothers" coming between them and "their" children. Many of them were very ready to condemn the mothers' ways of child-rearing. I often saw dummies taken away as "dirty", and small children forced to drink from a cup rather than their accustomed bottle because the ward sister decided the child was "too old" to have one.

The sad reality is that doctors and nurses at that time were ignorant of the harm caused by separating small children from their mothers. Very few doctors or nurses recognized that mothers and young children needed care as "a unit". It is interesting to recall that, at this time, aristocratic and well-to-do families rarely sent their children to hospital, so there was no issue of separation for them as those children were nursed at home and doctors attended them there. As a result of this, there was no opposition coming from families that might otherwise have had a more powerful voice.

How these changes came about

How these changes came about in spite of the huge opposition to them, I believe, was due to the lobbying having the nature of a "vertical pincer attack". At the "top" was the crucial research evidence already mentioned, by such figures as John Bowlby and James Robertson, with a few paediatricians such as Dermot McCarthy showing how keeping mothers and small children together on a ward could be done successfully. At the "bottom" were mothers with a massive desire for change, who knew instinctively that the research reflected their "truth". They wanted to be able to continue to be close and to care for their children when they were in hospital, alongside the professionals.

I think that the strength in the mothers to both start and maintain the battle came from a much bigger ground-swell of change in society following the Second World War. Women had made such a big contribution to that and the "old order" had changed. Women found their voice and were determined to use it.

The people in the middle of the "pincer" whose attitude needed to be changed the most were many doctors, nurses, and administrators. The concerted efforts of NAWCH were largely responsible for bringing about theses changes. NAWCH worked persuasively to get the doctors and gradually the government to respond to all the evidence provided by the Platt Report. Over the years that followed, many government guidelines were issued advising hospitals to make the changes needed with regard to parents staying in with small children and open visiting for all children. Play facilities with trained staff were all part of the same need to improve the quality of care and to recognize the emotional needs of the children and their parents.

Looking back now, it is impossible to say which of all these forces had the most profound influence. I believe it is the combination of them all that ultimately brought about the changes that, thankfully, are now taken for granted, though a "watchdog" role is still required and undertaken in some places by the renamed body of NAWCH (now Action for Sick Children).

My next field of helping to bring about change was with young women.

Contraception for the young

In 1969, I heard of some plans for a research study at the Birmingham Brook Advisory Centre. This was a pioneering centre offering contraception to the young for a very modest sum. At the time, the only other organization that offered women contraception was the Family Planning Association, which had been running for some years. To obtain contraception there, women had to provide proof that they were either married or were engaged to be married very soon. This led inevitably to subterfuge and the wearing of wedding rings by a few desperate unmarried women in order to get help.

The Brook Advisory Centres were set up by Robin and Helen Brook. They took a completely different view. They wanted to support young women who sought contraception (who, by then, could obtain the contraceptive pill) to do so in a way that would encourage them to take a responsible attitude to pregnancy. It was recognized that open access to the pill changed attitudes tremendously. Men were perceiving women suddenly as "sexually available" in ways they had not before, but also many women were thrown into conflicting feelings about its use. Birmingham Brook was determined to try to meet the needs of young women by offering privacy and time for all of them to talk with a social worker about the implications of seeking contraception, and advice from specially qualified doctors and nurses in choosing the best type of contraceptive for each woman.

I attended a Birmingham Brook's Research Committee meeting to examine the idea of my doing a research study. In spite of a diversity of views, it was eventually agreed that I should attempt

to discover the effect of the work of the Birmingham Brook Advisory Centre on its clients (Woodward, 1969). This felt like quite a tall
order. It needs to be appreciated that Brook was working at the
time, and for many years after, against an enormous tide of social
disapproval. Intermittently, we had to run the gauntlet of religious
groups praying for us on the pavement outside. We also had
constant hate mail telling us that we were doing "the devil's work",
and other similarly unpleasant things. Facts about the impact Brook
had on its clients were urgently needed.

A small grant was put together from two or three sources and
the study began with the Centre's receptionists inviting any client
who had attended for over a year, and who felt like contributing to
the study, to request an appointment with me. As more and more
of the clients shared their views, it became apparent that many of
them had enormous personal and social problems. When asked
why they had not felt able to bring these up on their return visits to
the doctors, three main inhibiting factors were frequently mentioned. The first was that the doctor's questions seemed to be
strictly limited to the clients' reactions to the contraceptive, hence
the number of doctors' notes stating "All well", or "Doing fine".
However, as soon as the clients could talk strictly confidentially to
me, many of them felt anything but "fine". Second, they felt that the
kind of problems they had were not sufficiently "medical" to
mention to a doctor, and many described how they felt unable to
embark on discussing something complicated with only ten
minutes available. Third, most of the doctors at that stage were
male, and many of the clients felt too shy to talk to them about
highly personal matters.

In 1970, the study was presented at a meeting of Brook staff and
other interested people, and it led to various changes. The biggest
change was the recognition that counselling was urgently needed
as an additional service. Soon after this, I was appointed as a social
worker with additional duties to set up and encourage counselling
for sexual and relational problems for Brook clients. Although at
this time there was a big ground-swell of increased openness about
sex, many young people felt unable to discuss it at home with their
parents. In response to this, Birmingham Brook set up an Educational Unit that produced a great deal of material for use in schools.
Some of this later met some fierce controversy.

The 1970s was an exciting time for psychosexual counselling, as a lot of information was becoming available, mostly from the USA (Kaplan, 1974; Masters & Johnson, 1970). They and many others were writing about how to help people with sexual problems in a serious way. Developing alongside Brook were new facilities for abortions under the new abortion laws, and Brook social workers were heavily involved in setting up pregnancy counselling to enable their clients to think through their choices with care.

Another field of work developed when infection testing clinics were started by one of the doctors who had specialized in venereology. This quickly came to fill a big demand, as the only other place that women could go for infection testing was the local venereal disease clinic, which was experienced as having a punitive atmosphere and carrying a very negative stigma.

Some of the clients complained bitterly that they had severe symptoms of vaginitis. These included constant discharge, vaginal soreness, and irritation, which for some of them was so severe it hurt them to sit down. Many of them were both bewildered and annoyed on being told there were no pathological findings. They would come to the reception desk saying, either angrily or near to tears, "The doctor says there's nothing the matter with me, but there is!" The venereologist had previously trained as a psychologist, and he decided that those clients who showed no signs of infection, but were complaining of symptoms, might be suffering from a psychosomatic form of vaginitis. He referred one or two of those clients to me.

As soon as they could accept that "psychosomatic" did not mean that their symptoms were imagined and an understanding of the pathologist's report (which to some of them looked like hieroglyphics) was shared with them, they began to tell their stories. It became clear that at a conscious level they wanted a sexual relationship with their partners, but that their bodies were saying "no" in response to deeper feelings of which they were either unaware or only partially aware. What was amazing to me was the rapidity with which the symptoms cleared as their conflicts became apparent to them. Then came a much longer task of discovering ways that they could resolve these. The Department of Health funded a research study for me to undertake and I benefited enormously from work done in the USA (Dodson & Friedrich, 1976). The findings of the research were published in a journal for GPs (Woodward, 1981).

It is interesting to examine why these young women were willing to work so co-operatively with me on these difficult conflicts when so many of them felt they had been treated as a "nuisance" by their GPs. Their doctors had offered them many different treatments, with inevitably ineffective results. Furthermore, hardly any of them were offered infection testing. Some of them had even had operations, and yet they had continued to suffer from their symptoms over many years. At Brook, some of the essentials of attachment were provided, in that the *availability* of help was immediate and ongoing, as they could contact me whenever they wanted. I also tried to be *responsive* to their individual needs, visiting some at home. Above all, I respected deeply both the situations they were in and how hard it was for some of them to recognize the emotional aspects of the condition and to work on some of their deeper psychological issues.

Overcoming the resistances

Some of the demands for changing attitudes to contraception were similar to those heard in seeking changes for children in hospitals, described earlier. The need to lessen unwanted pregnancies in the young was recognized at government level. There was also, as already mentioned, a huge demand for a service and a big change in attitude to sexual activity, particularly among the young, who were seeking greater freedom in a variety of ways. I believe an additional important factor was the role of certain individuals and small groups of people who took the initiative and made things happen at particular points in time. The level of resistance that had to be overcome by all of us working at Brook can most clearly be reflected in the "moral deficiency" diagnosis pronounced by psychiatrists many years earlier upon under-age pregnant girls. This led to many hundreds of them being incarcerated in hospitals *against their will*. It is a tragic and somewhat ironical fact that many of these girls, by then middle-aged women, were still languishing there so many years later, too institutionalized to leave, at the very time that Brook was starting up.

Therapy for women

In 1980, I left my post at Brook to work full-time in a ground-breaking new job with Birmingham Social Services. In the middle of the negotiations they suddenly clamped an embargo on all new posts, and I faced unemployment. I then took up an offer of a part-time position with a general practice, with a promise of funding that never materialized, in spite of the doctors referring many of their patients to me for counselling. I was very disappointed at the collapse of the Social Services post, but it gave me an unexpected opportunity to join a voluntary group of women. They, like me, had been excited at the setting up in London of a Women's Therapy Centre by Susie Orbach and Louise Eichenbaum. Many women at this time were spontaneously forming "consciousness raising" groups, questioning the role of women in society and being influenced by many feminist writers such as Jean Baker Miller (1976).

The group that I was in felt strongly that a change was needed in the mental health services for women. We were all highly critical of the current medical model and the way women were treated in psychiatric hospitals. The group began to give serious thought to how we might set up a women's therapy centre in Birmingham. There was a deep difference of opinion in the group about how such a centre could be funded. Another member of the group and I were determined that it should not be based on precarious grants such as those given to the Rape Crisis Centres and some Women's Refuges, where staff often worked voluntarily.

In 1982, after six years on a Community Health Council, I was appointed to Birmingham Central District Health Authority, which was responsible for all the teaching hospitals in the city. I was keen, as Chair of the Inner City Partnership Committee, that we should apply for a three-year grant with the hope of ultimately getting a women's therapy centre into the NHS. Others in the group saw this as "giving in to Big Brother". Gradually, we were able to persuade a majority of the group that the Establishment needed changing from within!

A carefully prepared project was put to the ICP Committee for funding. This was supported by the doctor who judged the applications on the grounds that he was "impressed by our perseverance"! Apparently he did not expect the group to stay working so long on the project while waiting for it to come to fruition. It took until 1984 before we were at last offered possible accommodation in what had originally been a flat rented from the city council by the health authority for a doctor's family. It had never been used, and when I went to see it I felt excited, knowing that once all the furniture was moved out it could make a very good place for a therapy centre to start. It was small and very easily accessed. We were able to furnish it with second-hand furniture, mostly from a nurses' home that was closing down, and gifts from friends and supporters. A huge amount of work followed. We had funding for two full-time posts, based on a low-grade administrator's scale, and a co-ordinator. We divided the posts into four to make a "team" and agonized over whom to appoint and how to plan ways of working that were acceptable to all of us.

The aim of the Centre was to offer counselling and therapy to women without any psychiatric labelling, or, in the first instance, a GP referral. Clients were offered a chance to take responsibility for their emotional distress and to discover ways of working to resolve their conflicts. The staff came with different theoretical backgrounds, but all held a feminist viewpoint, which simply meant that they offered the clients an understanding of their problems as women living in a patriarchal, racist, and ageist society. All clients were obliged to complete simplified forms of assessment both before and after therapy, and the centre had to produce annual reports, combined with a statistical analysis of the clients. The centre soon built up the inevitable waiting list, and we devised various ways of dealing with this. The staff grew in confidence and experience as we developed, by necessity, our own supervision groups. A researcher from Warwick University made a study of the Centre that was published some years later (McLeod, 1994).

In 1987, as we were hoping soon to be taken fully into the NHS as part of the Mental Health Section, there was a bizarre crisis. This arose when I received my usual monthly District Health Authority papers. I was horrified to see that the Chief Executive had put in a Resolution to "close all ICP projects". This was in response to a demand for a big cut in expenditure. I thought that that meant the end of The Women's Therapy Centre. I then recalled that, some months earlier, the Authority had passed a *Members'* Resolution that ICP projects were not to be cut, as the results in terms of money gained would be negligible. I knew that the chairman cared little about the Women's Therapy Centre, but also that he was an absolute stickler for protocol and would not agree to any administrator having the power to overturn a resolution taken by Members! I rushed out a memo to all Members reminding them of the earlier resolution, and went to the DHA meeting in a state of high anxiety. Outside, I saw the chairman, who gave me a curt nod. When the item came up, he announced that a Member had brought to his notice that a decision about the continuation of ICP projects had already been made, so he declared the item "null and void". I felt an overwhelming relief that the WTC could go on, and rushed off as soon as the meeting was over to let the other members of the centre know the good news.

In the following year, the centre was taken into the NHS, and we celebrated with a highly successful Feminist Therapists' Conference at a Birmingham University hall of residence. We had a beautiful poster printed to mark the occasion. Two years later, I retired from the Health Authority because of its impending closure, and in 1991 I was forced to retire from the Women's Therapy Centre on grounds of age. By that time I had been able to complete the first ever research study into the effect on twins of the loss of their twin and set up the Lone Twin Network. This was followed by a book (Woodward, 1998). My work on lone twins helped to deepen my understanding of how severe this particular loss can be.

Conclusion

When I look back to try to understand why all these projects met with such opposition, I can only confirm my view that each one was seen as subversive to some extent, as they challenged a particular power structure that those involved in were very unwilling to relinquish. The changes came about because enough people wanted them and a few were prepared to work against all odds to bring the changes about. There was also an element of chance, which meant that certain opportunities had been recognized and grasped at the time.

Having been personally involved in playing a small part in bringing about the changes described in this chapter, I believe it is vitally important to recognize the *nature* of the conflict involved.

Human beings have struggled for generations to challenge and overcome power structures that oppress people and block their attachment needs. Jean Baker Miller (1976) has written at length about this, highlighting the nature of the kind of "power-over" that is embedded in patriarchal societies and its particular negative effects on women's development. She believed that as human beings, men and women, we now urgently need a new meaning for "power". This must no longer be the "power-over" kind that requires others to be power*less*, but a form of mutual empowerment. This involves relating in ways that recognize everyone's attachment needs, and discovering compromises that can bring about positive changes.

In this country, we are seeing too many of our young people turning to binge drinking, expressing feelings of disillusionment, alienation, and, above all, violence, as shown in the knifings and shootings that are no longer a rarity in our schools and on our streets. We need to look at the stark choices before us and to challenge wherever we can the power structures, often based on a sense of ownership, that deny our attachment needs. We all need to do this in whatever spheres we are operating, at work or at home. I believe the future mental health and well-being of this country is at stake if we fail to do so.

References

Baker Miller, J. (1976). *Toward a New Psychology of Women*. London: Penguin.

Bowlby, J. (1979). *The Making and Breaking of Affectional Bonds*. London: Tavistock.

Bowlby, J. (1953). *Child Care and the Growth of Love*. London: Penguin.

Bowlby, J. (1998). *A Secure Base*. London: Routledge.

Dodson, M. G., & Friedrich, E. G. (1976). Psychosomatic vulvovaginitis. *Obstetrics & Gynecology*, J.51: 23 S.

Kaplan, H. (1974). *The New Sex Therapy*. New York: Brunner/Mazel.

Masters, W. H., & Johnson, U. F. (1970). *Human Sexual Inadequacy*. London: Churchill.

McLeod, E. (1994). *Women's Experience of Feminist Therapy and Counselling*. Buckingham: Open University Press.

Platt Report (1959). *The Welfare of Children in Hospital.* London: HMSO.

Robertson, J. (1953). *A Two-Year-Old Goes to Hospital.* Film.

Robertson, J. (1958). *Young Children in Hospital.* London: Tavistock.

Robertson, J. (1962). *Hospitals and Children.* London. Gollanz.

Woodward, J. (1959). Emotional disturbances of burned children. *British Medical Journal,* 1: 1009.

Woodward, J. (1962). Parental visiting of children with burns. *British Medical Journal,* II: 1656–1657.

Woodward J. (1969). *The Effect of the Work of Birmingham Brook Advisory Centre on its Clients.* Birmingham: FPA.

Woodward J. (1978). *Has Your Child Been in Hospital?* London: NAWCH.

Woodward J. (1981). The diagnosis and treatment of psychosomatic vulvovaginitis. *The Practitioner,* 225: 1673.

Woodward J. (1998). *The Lone Twin.* London. FAB.

Woodward, J., & Jackson, D. (1961). Emotional reaction in burned children and their mothers. *British Journal of Plastic Surgery, xiii*(4): 316.

INDEX